Getting Started in Charitable Gift Planning

Your Guide to Planned Giving

Brian M. Sagrestano, JD, CFRE
Robert E. Wahlers, MS, CFRE

D1737314

*Charity*Channel®
PRESS™

Getting Started in Charitable Gift Planning: Your Guide to Planned Giving

One of the **In the Trenches**™ series

Published by
CharityChannel Press, an imprint of CharityChannel LLC
424 Church Street, Suite 2000
Nashville, TN 37219 USA

CharityChannel.com

ISBN Print Book: 978-1-938077-85-2
Library of Congress Control Number: 2016950494

13 12 11 10 9 8 7 6 5 4 3 2 1

Printed in the United States of America

This and most CharityChannel Press books are available at special quantity discounts for bulk purchases for sales promotions, premiums, fundraising, or educational use. For information, contact CharityChannel Press, 424 Church Street, Suite 2000, Nashville, TN 37219 USA. +1 949-589-5938.

Publisher's Acknowledgments

This book was produced by a team dedicated to excellence; please send your feedback to Editors@ CharityChannel.com.

We first wish to acknowledge the tens of thousands of peers who call CharityChannel.com their online professional home. Your enthusiastic support for the **In the Trenches**™ series is the wind in our sails.

Members of the team who produced this book include:

Editors

Acquisitions: Linda Lysakowski

Comprehensive Editing: Stephen Nill

Copy Editing: Jill McLain

Production

Layout: Stephen Nill

Design: Deborah Perdue

Administrative

CharityChannel LLC: Stephen C. Nill, CEO

Marketing and Public Relations: John Millen

About the Authors

Brian M. Sagrestano, JD, CFRE

Brian is the president and founder of Gift Planning Development (GPD) LLC, a full-service gift planning consulting firm. He provides gift planning services to a wide range of charitable clients from national organizations focused on high-end philanthropic planning to local charities seeking to start new gift planning programs using his Planned Giving Essentials and Planned Giving In a Box programs. Some of his clients include the University of Notre Dame, Temple University, Create a Jewish Legacy, Harmony Foundation, Bassett Health, The Community Foundation of Herkimer and Oneida Counties, Inc., and Delaware Art Museum. In 2013, Gift Planning Development became a member firm in Constellation Advancement, LLC, a full-service fundraising consulting firm. Prior to starting GPD in 2007, Brian spent twelve years as a charitable gift planner, directing the programs for the University of Pennsylvania, Middlebury College, and Meridian Health Affiliated Foundations.

Brian is a nationally sought-after speaker on gift planning topics, keynoting or presenting at many conferences, including the National Conference on Philanthropic Planning, the National Conference on Planned Giving, the AFP International Conference on Fundraising, the American Council on Gift Annuities Conference, and the Crescendo Practical Planned Giving Conference, as well local and regional conferences around the country. He has taught thousands of fundraisers, professional advisors, board members, and philanthropists how to use a donor-focused approach to integrate philanthropic goals with tax, estate, and financial planning.

A regular contributor to Advancing Philanthropy, Planned Giving Today, Planned Giving Mentor, PlannedGiving.Com, and Planned Giving Tomorrow, Brian has also been cited in numerous publications, including CASE Currents and the Chronicle of Philanthropy. He and Robert coauthored *The Philanthropic Planning Companion—The Fundraisers' and Professional Advisors' Guide to Charitable Gift Planning* (Wiley 2012), the 2013 AFP–Skystone Partners prize winner for research in philanthropy.

Brian is a past board member of the Partnership for Philanthropic Planning (PPP), the Gift Planning Council of New Jersey, and PPP of Greater Philadelphia, as well as a past member of the editorial board of the *Journal of Gift Planning.*

An honors graduate of both Cornell University and Notre Dame Law School, Brian lives with his wife and four children in New Hartford, New York, the scenic gateway to the Adirondack Mountains. In his off hours, Brian sings with the Mohawk Valley Chapter of the Barbershop Harmony Society, an internationally ranked barbershop chorus, as well as his local church choir. He also likes to spend time outdoors, hiking, canoeing, kayaking, and skiing in the Adirondack Park.

To learn more about GPD, Constellation or to share your thoughts with Brian, visit *giftplanningdevelopment.com* or email brian@giftplanningdevelopment.com.

Robert E. Wahlers, MS, CFRE

Robert is the Vice President of Development for Meridian Health Affiliated Foundations, where he oversees the gift planning, annual giving and grants development program for the eight hospitals in the Meridian Health System. During his tenure, he has also served as the Executive Director for Jersey Shore University Medical Center Foundation and K. Hovnanian Children's Hospital. Over his more than twenty-five-year-career, Robert has worked in the financial and estate planning field and in the nonprofit sector with the Boy Scouts of America, the American Cancer Society, Virtua Foundation, and now Meridian Health. Robert learned early on the value of developing relationships with professional advisors and honed those skills while with the American Cancer Society, where he saw how philanthropic planning can be an asset for the donor and the charity.

A speaker to audiences of five to five thousand, Robert has presented at such conferences as the National Conference on Philanthropic Planning, the National Conference on Planned Giving, the Association of Fundraising Professionals International Conference, the Boy Scouts of America All Hands Conference, and the American Cancer Society Distinguished Gifts Conference, as well as several regional and local conferences.

Robert is an honors graduate with a master of science degree in human development and leadership with a concentration in nonprofit management from Murray State University and a bachelor of arts degree in psychology from Muhlenberg College. Robert and Brian coauthored their first book, *The Philanthropic Companion—The Fundraisers' and Professional Advisors' Guide to Charitable Gift Planning,* which was published by Wiley in 2012 and is the 2013 winner of the AFP–Skystone Partners Research Award. He has also been published in *Advancing Philanthropy* and *Planned Giving Today* and has been cited in the *Nonprofit Times,* the *Chronicle of Philanthropy,* and *Advancing Philanthropy,* among others. Robert serves on the faculty at Columbia University in its masters of fundraising management program.

He is a former national board member with the Partnership for Philanthropic Planning (PPP) and is active on several AFP committees. Robert also served on the boards of the Gift Planning Council of New Jersey and the Association of Fundraising Professionals–New Jersey Chapter, where he is a past president. Robert is also active as a 32nd degree York Rite and Scottish Rite Mason and Shriner.

When not working, Robert spends time with his wife and two children at their home at the Jersey Shore or on the Inner Banks of North Carolina. He also enjoys racing wooden sailboats as part of the Barnegat Bay Yacht Racing Association and maintains a studio for illustration and oil painting.

Dedication

To the organizations where we served that inspired us through their missions and gave us the opportunity to work with extraordinary donors who make a lasting difference.

Authors' Acknowledgments

Having already written a comprehensive book on philanthropic planning, our second book and the resource book that supports it are allowing us to get back to the basics that we learned at the early stages of our careers.

All who enter into fundraising need to establish a baseline of knowledge that can serve them throughout their careers. We are both fortunate that our upbringing and values along with our education and early experience prepared us well to absorb the wisdom of those we were fortunate to meet—Diane McConnell, Ben Madonia, Jere Williams, Bill Davis, Bob Sharpe, Jr., Kathryn Miree, Ron Brown, Frank Congilose, Paul Hansen, Charles Schultz, Laura Fredricks, Bill Sturtevant, and Steve Simmonds—each who influenced our development and pointed us on the path toward building our expertise.

We have also been inspired by thousands of donors who were moved by the missions of the organizations we have served and put their faith and trust in us to help them in making gifts to support the Boy Scouts of America, Clarkson University, the American Cancer Society, Middlebury College, Virtua Foundation, Meridian Health Affiliated Foundations and the University of Pennsylvania.

We would like to thank the three gift planners who completed peer reviews of our manuscripts, including Roger Ellison, CFP, Johni Hays, JD, and Kristen Schultz Jaarda, JD. Their thoughtful comments and edits improved the content and flow of these materials. We would also like to thank Stephen Nill, JD, and the team at CharityChannel Press for their help and support throughout the process of putting this book together. Finally, we appreciate the review and thoughtful Foreword by Professor Russell James who continues to lead our field with his outstanding research to support gift planning and fundraising.

We are hopeful that ***Getting Started in Charitable Gift Planning: Your Guide to Planned Giving*** and the associated ***Getting Started in Charitable Gift Planning: Resource Book*** will be a guide to others as they grow in their knowledge to build relationships and assist the donors they serve.

Contents

Summary of Chapters

Gift Planning in the Twenty-First Century. Gift planning is a rapidly evolving area of the fundraising field. The needs and expectations of your prospects have fundamentally changed, which requires you to have a gift planning program and use it to help your prospects integrate their philanthropy into their overall tax, estate, and financial planning.

Are You Ready for Gift Planning? Before launching a gift planning program, ensure that your nonprofit is ready. Do not jump to the end—build a sound program on a solid foundation with appropriate infrastructure, prospect interaction, and marketing.

Culture of Donor-focused Gift Planning. A culture of donor-focused philanthropy should be the goal for every organization. It is a culture that synergistically motivates giving and investment by those tied to your organization's mission because you are invested in helping them craft a meaningful legacy that integrates their philanthropy into their overall planning.

Your Role in Gift Planning. Each member of the nonprofit team has a valuable role in making the gift planning program successful. In a donor-focused gift planning program, collaboration with colleagues is directly related to the success that can be achieved.

Performance Goals. Individual goals, objectives, and performance metrics based on activities, such as relationship building, donor cultivation, and stewardship, will be the most effective measures of the progress of your gift planning effort.

The Role of Your Board. Educating your board and enlisting its help will build your gift planning program by engaging board members along with others in the mission of your organization.

The Role of Volunteers. A successful volunteer program will bring your best donors closer to your organization and cultivate wonderful relationships with future donors. A weak volunteer program will alienate your best donors and make it less likely that prospects will invest in your mission.

The Role of Professional Advisors. Professional advisors are key members of the gift planning team. The most significant gifts involve a partnership among you, the donor, and the donor's professional advisors.

Identifying Gift Planning Prospects. Gift planning prospects are drawn from your regular, consistent donors known as "loyals." Gift planning prospects typically do not show up in wealth screenings and do not see themselves as wealthy.

Approaching Your Prospects. One-on-one visits are the best way to build donor relationships that lead to planned gifts. It may take many cultivation visits before you can make a solicitation, but be sure each one is purposeful and moves the relationship forward.

Soliciting Prospects. Gift planning conversations with high-end donors require a philanthropic planning approach, which will frequently result in a gift with annual, major, and planned gift components.

Concierge Stewardship. Effective stewardship starts by tying your donors to your mission through outcomes-based stories that cement the connection between philanthropy and results.

Marketing in a Donor-focused Way. Traditional gift planning marketing is no longer effective due to changing donor demographics and the proliferation of canned gift planning materials that try to do too much. Targeted marketing to identified gift planning prospects on a moves management platform has the highest likelihood of success.

Marketing to Everyone. Gift planning marketing starts at the top of the gift planning pyramid, but if you do not market to all levels, your program will not be sustainable.

Marketing to Identified Prospects. Because there are too many loyals to visit, gift planning marketing helps you reach this group.

Marketing to Major and Principal Prospects. Do not use mass marketing of gift planning with your high-net-worth prospects. Instead, have a conversation with each high-net-worth donor to suggest when gift planning might be appropriate to meet their personal planning and charitable goals.

Sector-specific Gift Planning Tips. Each fundraising sector has unique challenges in building gift planning programs. These challenges can be identified and overcome with planning.

The Time Is Now. Information is useful only if you use the knowledge that you gain. Take what you have before you and apply it to your development practice.

Foreword

Based on their previous excellent work, I greatly anticipated the opportunity to read *Getting Started in Charitable Gift Planning* and the accompanying *Getting Started in Charitable Gift Planning: Resource Book* (the *Resource Book*) from Brian Sagrestano and Robert Wahlers. I can now say that—just as I suspected—I am once again really pleased with their fine work. I think you will be too.

Of course, there have been other books on charitable gift planning. Some deal intricately with the technicalities of trusts and taxes. Some pontificate on marketing philosophies. Some share research statistics and demographics. Some even look at the brains of donors (my personal favorite). Each of these resources can be useful at different points, but there is often a risk that readers will become overwhelmed and, ultimately, change very little about what they actually do.

These books by Brian and Robert are different. Yes, they can serve as a great reference resource for practicing fundraisers. But what makes this set so outstanding is that it simply and clearly answers the most important question: "What should I do next?" For practicing fundraisers, that is usually the only question that really matters *right now*.

Brian and Robert condense their years of successful experience with many organizations and translate it into a comprehensive, yet readable, guide that always answers "What should I do next?" Whether you are new to the field or have years of experience, their perspectives will help you to work on the *right* projects for *right now*.

A practical and effective set of specific instructions like those found in these two books is particularly important for success in this field. Why? Because gift planning is *different*. Consider this. Suppose you start soliciting current gifts by direct mail. You start with a list and write a letter. Very soon, you will learn exactly how successful (or unsuccessful) your approach was. You immediately get dollars in the door (or not). You can quickly learn, improve, and readjust. Expert advice is nice, but you could probably figure out the basics just by trial and error.

Gift planning, especially for bequest gifts, is different. You could still start with a list and write a letter. If all goes perfectly well, you will start to see bequest dollars in the door in . . . a few years—or perhaps decades. Unfortunately, in gift planning you can do things exactly wrong for a very long time and never know the difference. That's why expert advice—like that given here—is so critical for success.

Despite the difficulties of delayed dollars, the promise of gift planning is simply too great to ignore. Take any nonprofit organization and compare the money spent on fundraising for specific types of gifts (e.g., from direct mail, phone calls, events, major gifts, or bequest gifts) with the money actually received. I have yet to see an organization where bequest gifts weren't dramatically more cost effective than any other type of fundraising—and by a massive margin. The returns from investments can be enormously attractive. But the delay can be challenging. Other fundraisers just have to raise money. Gift planners have to make their case to boards and executive directors, establish goals and metrics, and still make time to work with donors. Navigating those complicated waters becomes much easier with a resource like this.

Finally, *Getting Started in Charitable Gift Planning* and the *Resource Book* provide a great reference for understanding and explaining complex gifts. The problem with some other references on complex gifts is that they are so complicated that even if you did successfully digest the information—much of which you wouldn't need unless you were a practicing attorney drafting legal documents—you might actually become less successful in communicating with donors. Complexity is great for tax attorneys drafting documents. But complexity when communicating with donors can kill both interest and motivation. These volumes explain the gifts, but they explain them in ways that help you, in turn, effectively explain them to donors. These books are, once again, ultimately practical.

I hope you will enjoy these volumes as much as I have. But most of all, I hope you take the authors' closing advice: "Information is useful only if you use the knowledge that you gain. Take what you have before you and apply it to your development practice."

Russell James, JD, PhD, CFP®

Professor and Director of Graduate Studies in Charitable Financial Planning

Texas Tech University, Lubbock, Texas

Author of *Visual Planned Giving: An Introduction to the Law & Taxation of Charitable Gift Planning; Inside the Mind of the Bequest Donor: A Visual Presentation of the Neuroscience and Psychology of Effective Planned Giving Communication*; and *American Charitable Bequest Demographics (1992–2012)*

Introduction

With the hustle and bustle of our daily lives, it can be easy to just go through the motions and not ever pause to reflect. When taking a journey, whether for business or for pleasure, there is an opportunity to stop and think about things in a whole new way, to reflect about the path you are on—the why, the how, and what can be done to improve.

On a recent trip with my family to the Great Smoky Mountains National Park, we took a hike to find a waterfall. It is a good goal for young children. As you walk along the rugged trail, you can lose your footing if you are not careful. You are encouraged onward at first by the idea that you will see something new based on the description that was explained by the park ranger, but then once you get underway, you are urged onward by the sights that continue to surprise you and then, as you near the destination, by the sound of the falls as you hear the water dropping on the rocks and into the pool below. It is a beautiful vision. We do not always get a great reward, but if you keep following the trail, you are bound to see something and can at least enjoy the company of those who are along the journey with you. And while you may enjoy a physical experience of a mountain hike, sometimes it is the mental challenge and the new knowledge that are equally uplifting.

Getting Started in Charitable Gift Planning will offer you a map for your hike into charitable gift planning. With knowledge as your reward, you can start out on the trail and learn and understand how to be donor-focused in your approach and how to reach your destination where gifts can flow like a waterfall. And do not worry if you haven't packed all that you need; the accompanying *Getting Started in Charitable Gift Planning Resource Book* has all the tools for what you might encounter. Like the hike in the mountains of North Carolina, it can be more fun when you experience it with others, so let us encourage you to share the information you learn so that it can become a part of your new dialogue with colleagues and donors. Like any journey, it starts with taking that first step . . . and by reading this book, you are on your way.

On the same trip, we stopped in to visit the Museum of the Cherokee Indian in Cherokee, North Carolina.

A well-done but simple museum that does a fine job with its information and exhibits to convey the chronology of the indigenous people who inhabited North America as early as 11,000 BC, we learned about Paleo man and the evolution of tools and the use of natural resources.

From Paleo Man to Planned Giving . . .

Paleo Indians were the first people in North America. Groups made up of several families moved seasonally to gather wild plant foods and hunt animals, including many now-extinct Ice Age mammals, like the mastodon. Although little evidence remains, they probably lived in lean-to shelters or took advantage of naturally occurring caves and overhangs.

Over the next seven thousand years, as food gathering became more efficient, Archaic Indians were able to develop more sophisticated tools, including the atlatl for hunting and weighted nets for fishing. Mega fauna, such as the woolly mammoth, became extinct, and smaller animals like the white-tailed deer became an important source of food. In the late Archaic Period, Indians began to cultivate plants like the bottle gourd and squash. Both were productive and easy to grow, and gourds were also used as containers.

During the next six hundred years, people developed a new variety of corn called eastern flint, which closely resembles modern corn. It was grown with beans and squash in fields surrounded by gourd birdhouses hung on poles. These provided homes for purple martins, birds that eat destructive insects and keep crows and blackbirds away from the corn. The increased food supply provided leisure time, which people used to build mounds, refine arts and crafts (and create new art forms like shell gorgets), and celebrate religious ceremonies.

So at our essence, humankind requires basic needs—food, shelter, and tools. Before we can develop, we must first make sure that our basic needs are met. What are the essentials of gift planning? Like the early inhabitants that dealt with life in a very different way than we do today, what challenges exist in your life? As a fundraiser, do you have what you need to serve your organization? Have you evolved to be donor-focused, or are you still putting the needs of your charity first? In our award-winning first book, *The Philanthropic Planning Companion* (Wiley 2012), we describe the evolution from basic gifts to planned giving to gift planning and now philanthropic planning. Where do you lie along that progression in your thoughts? Do you understand the tools of gift planning? With that knowledge, have you learned to approach your donors respecting their needs to determine what is best or are you still trying to sell them on the idea of a will or charitable gift annuity? And if you have mastered the use of donor-focused gift planning, have you learned about philanthropic planning and the benefits of segmenting your approach to your wealthiest and most engaged donors?

Building the Infrastructure

As fundraisers, we can attend classes, seminars, or conferences and gain knowledge in a new area of fundraising, but implementing strategic ideas and turning them into useful programs can be daunting. *Getting Started in Charitable Gift Planning* will cover the steps needed to move an organization from one that has focused on annual and major giving to one that can include gift planning and have it serve as an integrated component of its development program. The accompanying *Getting Started in Charitable Gift Planning Resource Book* (*Resource Book*) will include basic tools and templates to create the infrastructure necessary to start a gift planning program.

Interacting with Prospects

Getting Started in Charitable Gift Planning and the *Resource Book* will provide fundraisers and nonprofits with the basics of how to identify gift planning prospects and opportunities, have the gift planning conversation, and steward gift planning donors, including our groundbreaking work applying generational cohorts to fundraising strategies. It will also define the different gift planning tools and how to apply them to particular prospect situations. Whether meeting with donors or their professional advisors, fundraisers need the ability to speak the same language and understand the core concepts.

Marketing the Opportunities

Key to the success of a gift planning program is a donor-focused gift planning marketing effort. Brian first introduced this idea back in 2007, and it has changed the way charities approach gift planning marketing. *Getting Started in Charitable Gift Planning* will provide a wealth of gift planning marketing ideas to approach everyone in the nonprofit's database right up to the highest level identified gift planning prospects. It will illustrate a marketing approach tailored to today's donors.

Together, *Getting Started in Charitable Gift Planning* and the accompanying *Resource Book* will guide you as you start your journey to build a great gift planning program. Just as Paleo man had to evolve from a hunter-gatherer to a farmer, your program will evolve, starting with the basics of building infrastructure, working with prospects, and marketing your program. Over time, you will add the components of a *stage two* program, which assists your prospects and donors in meeting personal planning objectives while supporting your nonprofit. And when you are ready, you will add philanthropic planning to create a *stage three* gift planning program, which involves helping your prospects and donors integrate their philanthropy into their overall tax, estate, and financial planning using complex assets and all of the tools in the gift planning toolbox.

Part One

Getting Started in Charitable Gift Planning

To build a donor-focused gift planning program, you need to understand what it is, why it is important to your prospects, how it fits into your overall fundraising program, and most importantly, whether your nonprofit should be pursuing it. In **Part One**, we walk you through how to answer these questions, including how to draft your internal case to convince current leadership and sustain the program into the future.

Chapter One

Gift Planning in the Twenty-First Century

In This Chapter

- ···➔ Why gift planning is important for your prospects

- ···➔ The role of gift planning within the overall fundraising program

- ···➔ The case for gift planning

- ···➔ Sustaining the gift planning program into the future

Gift planning is a young and changing field. In its short history, it has also been known as deferred giving, planned giving, legacy giving, future giving, and philanthropic planning. Originally focused on obtaining gifts from the elderly and wealthy, it now focuses on those engaged by the mission of the nonprofit, commonly referred to as "loyals," and assisting them in creating gifts that meet the long-term needs of the donors and the nonprofits. As the field has evolved, a broad range of practitioners working in both the nonprofit and for-profit sectors have become involved in helping philanthropists create legacies. At the same time, it has become clear that charitable mission is the true motivator of charitable gifts, not the tools, gift vehicles, or tax benefits of making these gifts.

The turbulent economic circumstances of recent years and changes in the generational makeup of the donor population have substantially altered the gift planning landscape. While we served on the board of The National Committee on Planned Giving, we were involved in the adoption of the organization's new name, the Partnership for Philanthropic Planning, reflecting these fundamental changes in the industry. Unfortunately, there is limited literature explaining the implications of these changes, and most of the writings on gift planning are out of date, based upon a decades-old model.

The traditional approach has served the sector well, but there is now a need for the next step in the evolution of gift planning. Over the last twenty-five years, we have worked closely with professional advisors and fundraisers. We have had successes and failures, learned from our mistakes, and honed our skills in the field. Our formal education provided the foundation, while our experience has allowed us to amass an understanding of the many different perspectives on philanthropy. We have met and nurtured relationships with donors and advisors and have become accustomed to the differing personalities

Donor-focused Gift Planning

Gift planning is a powerful and meaningful way for individuals to give to charities, ensure their long-term futures, and also meet personal planning objectives. It is the process of cultivating, designing, facilitating, and stewarding gifts. Gift planning uses a variety of financial tools and techniques for giving. It usually requires the assistance of one or more qualified specialists, utilizes tax incentives that encourage charitable giving when appropriate, covers the full spectrum of generosity by individuals and institutions, and is based on powerful traditions of giving in the United States.

 Definition

and the varying motivations that shape the discussions around philanthropic planning.

As we are now required to recognize the needs of the latest generations of donors, the New Philanthropists (born 1946 to the present), the donor-focused gift planning model provides a necessary approach.

We have written this book for the fundraisers looking to understand planned giving as they have heard it, but then improved upon that term and concept to give you an appreciation for donor-focused gift planning and introduce you to the concept of philanthropic planning so that if you decide to continue on your journey and quest for the summit, you can take the next step to *The Philanthropic Planning Companion*.

The techniques of charitable gift planning include both revocable and irrevocable arrangements, gifts available for use at the time they are given, gifts that may not be available until a future date, and split-interest gifts intended to balance financial, personal, and charitable objectives.

Donors should seek charitable gift planning advice from professionals with integrity, expertise, and experience in law, investments, property, tax, and charitable transfers to ensure the technical merits of the transfer and the philanthropic quality of the gift. Similarly, fundraisers should look to work with professional advisors to assist them in their work with donors.

Why Gift Planning Is Important for Your Prospects

Donor-focused philanthropy is an emerging model for raising funds. Instead of asking what donors can do for nonprofits, it asks what donors need to accomplish for themselves, their families, and their future. It seeks what is really important to them in their lives, including the legacy they want to build. It then asks how nonprofits they support can be integrated into their tax, estate, and financial planning to help meet these present and future goals. It requires your organization to develop

Paying for Grandchildrens' College

One of my charitable gift annuity donors has enjoyed the regular income from a $100,000 gift annuity that she and her late husband started many years ago. When she recently hinted she was considering another gift, we again talked about a charitable gift annuity, but I was also sure to ask her what was important for her. She said that since her son had passed away, helping her three youngest grandchildren pay for college was keeping her awake at night. She shared that she still holds highly appreciated stock in a company in which her husband was an executive that would be subject to high capital gains taxes if she sold it. I explained how she could donate the stock and we could use it to establish a new college education gift annuity that would help cover college tuition over the next eight years, enabling her grandkids to go to college.

—Robert

 **stories from the real world**

significant relationships with your donors to understand what impact they want to have today, what outcomes they hope to achieve for tomorrow, and what legacy they desire to create during their lifetimes and beyond.

Donor-focused gift planning provides donors with the ability to meet both their personal planning objectives and their philanthropic goals to craft a more meaningful and lasting legacy. To achieve this goal, you need to partner with your donors and their advisors, listen to what is important to them, and provide the appropriate tools and support to help them reach this end. In **Part Three,** we'll discuss why the model has changed and how to identify which prospects are open to different types of gift planning messages.

The Role of Gift Planning within the Overall Fundraising Program

There is an old adage in financial planning circles that "people don't plan to fail; they fail to plan." And while death is certain, we know that statistically two out of every three people die without a valid will.

How I Broke the Ice with Humor

Early on in my gift planning career, I discovered that most prospects do not want to deal with the issue of their own mortality. Trying to convince them to discuss the topic wasn't going to work, so I developed other language, such as "at your passing," "when you no longer need these assets," "at the end of a very long life," and "when your legacy is fulfilled." Usually these types of conversations got the prospect into the conversation. In one instance, I was speaking to a wealthy couple in their early nineties who had not yet written their wills because "that wasn't necessary yet." As the conversation progressed, the wife said to me, "Now, if I die, then I would no longer need these assets and can fulfill my legacy, correct?" I felt good that she adopted some of language and was acknowledging that she would eventually pass and it might be time to write her will. At the same time, I could still sense that reticence to discuss the topic, so I introduced a little humor and asked her, "If you die?" She looked up at me, let out a hearty laugh, and responded, "When I die." They then went on to make the gift.

—Brian

 stories from the real world

---

Nationally, 80 percent of all planned gifts come in the form of nonprofits being named as the beneficiary of a will, living trust, donor-advised fund, life insurance policy, retirement plan, payable-on-death account (for bank assets), or transfer-on-death account (for investment assets and real estate). As a result, much of the effort for most gift planning programs is focused on encouraging these types of gifts. The reality is that a large percentage of this effort is wasted on "people who fail to plan." Wouldn't it be better to identify the prospects who are most likely to actually plan and include your nonprofit in those plans? If you do, you'll find that gift planning receipts can climb to 25 to 40 percent of your total individual gifts revenue.

A recent study by the Center on Philanthropy at Indiana University shows that the average annual gift will double once a planned gift is put in place, largely because the donor has elevated the nonprofit to the status of a family member and has a much greater investment in the nonprofit's success. Because these gifts mature in the future, donors typically dedicate them to endowment. Frequently they endow programs donors supported during their lifetimes with annual gifts. The most sophisticated charities in the country rely on planned gift revenue to secure their future. The most sophisticated donors rely upon gift planning to create or enhance their legacies.

For charities without gift planning programs, too much of their success (or failure) is based on annual giving where special events and direct mail form the basis of their fundraising. Major giving is relative to the development of their donors, but often they stop there in their cultivation of gifts.

Rule of Thirds

The rule of thirds has many applications. The basic rule is that one out of every three prospects will give you the amount you request. To get to those prospects, you have to apply the rule in reverse. So how many prospects does it take to get your gift? By applying the rule, the answer is twenty-seven. You start by calling twenty-seven prospects, of which nine agree to take your visit. Of those nine, three are actually interested, and eventually you cultivate them to the point of asking them to make an investment in an area of your nonprofit that is important to them. One of the three makes a gift of the amount you request. This can be a lot of rejection, particularly for new fundraisers. But as you get better at it, your results will improve.

Many veterans of gift planning know all too well that most CEOs or executive directors can get stuck in annual giving with direct mail campaigns or special events with the glitz and visual appeal of proving to untrained board members or volunteers that they are *doing something* even though the cost to raise a dollar can be fifty cents or more. And while these activities are important to donor acquisition and need to be part of the overall fundraising program, the return on philanthropic investment (RPI) should be calculated and tracked so they are managed in line with the development strategy.

Similarly, inexperienced board members and fundraisers often look to corporations and foundations as the best prospects for gifts. They have set systems for applying for grants, and if a gift request is denied, it is done at a distance, through the mail, so the nonprofit does not have to face rejection directly. However, when you look at national statistics, corporations and foundations make up a very small part of the dollars raised by nonprofits. The vast majority of gifts come from individuals, which is where your nonprofit should focus its attention. We are not saying this is easy. In fact, professional fundraisers are paid to be told no and are taught the rule of thirds. If you are hitting .300 as a fundraiser (to use a baseball analogy), you are going to the Hall of Fame.

For those who have been able to see a forest regenerate and come back to life after a fire, you see vegetation in the form of ferns poking up through the ashes as nature heals itself. This leads to pine saplings that grow to create a canopy to shield the floor from direct sunlight to allow oaks and maples to establish themselves in the cool shade and grow even taller until one day the "hard woods" take over and rule the forest while the "soft woods" fall into a lesser role.

This evolving process over many years can be a wonderful example of a successful development model.

AG (annual gifts) = ferns and mosses

MG (major gifts) = pines

PG (planned gifts) = oaks and maples

All are necessary to sustain the forest, and without the ferns and mosses, you never get to the pines and certainly would find it hard to ever expect oaks and maples. Still, given the lack of understanding of many in the sector, they "can't see the forest through the trees," as the saying goes.

Nonprofits that have only annual giving programs will have a hard time growing their forests. More sophisticated nonprofits have discovered the value of major giving in their programs, where effort with fewer qualified wealthier constituents can yield bigger gifts at a tremendously lower cost to raise a dollar but, more appropriately, a better RPI. This leads us to planned giving.

If AG = 1X

And MG = 10X

Then PG = 100X

These values have been considered to be the typical expectation of an interested and engaged donor who might make regular annual gifts but could then be cultivated to make major gifts and eventually an ultimate planned gift that could be a hundred times the initial annual giving level.

So if you focus your efforts on individuals and segment those capable of making substantial gifts, you can put your limited and valuable resources toward what might deliver the greatest RPI.

You need then to ask yourself if you can be patient enough to grow your forest from ferns to pines to oaks? As fundraisers, can we present an internal case for support that will transform the culture of our organization to sustain the program through several leadership changes in CEOs and board chairs?

The Case for Gift Planning

Gift planning is a major organizational commitment. You are adding a new area to your fundraising effort. In the current environment, gift planning is typically found as part of the individual gifts effort, which often includes annual, major, and principal gifts.

Most individual giving programs start with annual giving (usually also involving fundraising events), which is designed to encourage individuals to provide regular support each year. More sophisticated annual giving efforts have moved away from most events and focus on outright gifts, often payable monthly or by payroll deduction. In today's philanthropic environment with over 90 percent of the dollars coming from fewer than 10 percent of the donors, major giving becomes the best source of support. Major gift programs develop more meaningful relationships with higher-net-worth prospects who are able to make more significant commitments to the organization, and can utilize multiyear pledges. The most sophisticated individual giving programs add a principal gifts or philanthropic planning program to work with the top 1 percent of prospects. These programs, which we cover in much greater detail in our book, *The Philanthropic Planning Companion: The Fundraisers' and Professional Advisors' Guide to Charitable Gift Planning* (Wiley 2012), work with prospects capable of making transformative gifts and help those individuals create meaningful philanthropic plans for

---

Lesson Learned: Stay in Touch with Donors

When I took over the gift planning program at the University of Pennsylvania, the gift planning staff had been reduced over a period of several years from ten to four members. During my tenure, we rebuilt and enhanced the effort, so when I left, the team had fourteen people. During the time we were rebuilding the staff, we attempted to call upon many of the loyal Harrison Society members (Penn's legacy society) and were rebuffed. It took the better part of four years and regular consistent mail, phone, and email contact to get these donors to agree to visits. When we surveyed them as to why, the members said that they didn't feel their gifts were important, since no one had been in touch for such a long time. Many of them had removed Penn from their estate plans as a result. We learned that we needed to do a better job sustaining the gift planning effort if we wanted to see those gifts mature for the benefit of the university.

—Brian

 stories from the real world

themselves and their families now and into the future. In most cases, organizations will build annual, major, gift planning and principal/philanthropic planning programs in that order.

The number-one reason we see gift planning programs fail (together we have launched over seventy-five of them and reviewed dozens more) is a lack of organizational commitment. To overcome this challenge, we have developed an *internal* case for support. This case documents why your organization is building a gift planning program and why it needs to be sustained consistently over time. It is covered in detail in Chapter Six of the *Resource Book*, including a sample case. If you do not sustain your program, it will not produce the gifts you desire.

To Recap

◆ Gift planning is a rapidly evolving part of the fundraising field.

◆ The needs and expectations of your prospects have fundamentally changed, which requires you to have a gift planning program and use it to help your prospects to integrate their philanthropy into their overall tax, estate, and financial planning.

◆ Gift planning is a key element of your individual gifts program.

◆ Over five to ten years, once it has a chance to mature, a well-built gift planning program can produce 25 to 40 percent of the revenue of your individual gifts effort.

◆ Once you start a gift planning program, you need to sustain it or your lapsed gift planning donors will be very difficult to reengage.

Chapter Two

Are You Ready for Gift Planning?

In This Chapter

- ⋯➔ Are you ready for gift planning?

- ⋯➔ Readiness assessment

- ⋯➔ The legs of the gift planning stool: infrastructure, prospect interaction, and marketing

- ⋯➔ Is your mission statement relevant and will it be lasting?

Knowing that gift planning is important for your prospects and will be valuable to your organization, it is time to ask if you are ready to start a proactive gift planning program. In some cases, you may think that you have a program already, but if you really consider it, you may find that you are not fully engaged in all that is necessary for success.

Over the last several years, Brian, working with Viken Mikalean and his team at *PlannedGiving.com*, developed a readiness assessment. The results will reveal a lot about your organization and whether you are indeed ready to take the next step.

We recommend that you start by filling out the assessment on the next page for yourself. Then ask other professionals on your staff team, lay volunteers, and board members to fill it out. By enlisting the feedback of others involved in your nonprofit and averaging the scores, you will generate the best profile of your gift planning readiness.

Evaluating Your Scores

If your average score is more than 50, *Congratulations*! Your nonprofit is well positioned to pursue gift planning. If the average score is between 30 and 50, you have some work to do but remain a good candidate for gift planning. If your average score is less than 30, you should focus on other components of your nonprofit so that you are ready to launch a gift planning program in the future.

A word of warning: If all of your scores are near perfect, meaning everyone rates your nonprofit near 100, it is time to look again. The tool is only as accurate as the data. We've worked with hundreds of nonprofits and there has never been a perfect score.

Readiness Assessment

In the spaces provided, indicate the degree to which you agree with the following statements, on a scale of 1 to 10, with 1 being "I disagree completely" and 10 being "I agree completely."

_____ We have a mission statement.

_____ Our mission will still be relevant in fifty to a hundred years.

_____ We have a compelling need for charitable support to sustain our mission.

_____ We have an effective strategic plan to implement our mission.

_____ Our staff and board leadership are interested in pursuing long-term support.

_____ We are financially stable.

_____ We pursue endowments to ensure our long-term future.

_____ We regularly garner support from individuals.

_____ We have a group of loyal donors who have supported us in the recent past.

_____ We have one hour per week for the next year to invest in gift planning.

_____Total Score

Note: An electronic version of this assessment is available at *areyoureadyforplannedgiving.com.*

!
important

Ensuring Accuracy

If you are concerned that your numbers are not accurate, the first step is to ask more people to complete the assessment. The more participants you include in the evaluation process, the more it balances your scores. If you do not have more people to participate, remove the outliers from the survey. You know the ones we're talking about—the people who gave you all "1" or all "10" scores on every statement.

For you statistics experts, or if you just like to play with numbers, you can weight answers given to specific questions by your colleagues in specific departments. For example, when someone from your Finance Department gives you an answer to statement six about financial stability, you can give that answer greater weight because that's the person's field. Similarly, you can give greater weight to the answers you get from members of the board about how interested they themselves are in gift planning (statement five).

A third strategy is to create average scores for each statement. This will allow you to zero in on the areas where you need the greatest improvement and address them first.

How Do We Use the Readiness Data?

The average from the assessment is not a *final score* but rather a snapshot of where your organization is now in relation to where you want to be. To help you improve your readiness in each area, we have repeated the individual readiness assessment statements below and included a more detailed discussion of how to increase your readiness for that area.

1. We have a mission statement.

    This statement is intended to address:

    ◆ whether your organization, in fact, has a mission statement;

    ◆ whether personnel within the organization are aware of it; and

    ◆ whether said personnel are conversant with it.

To improve your score, compose a mission statement if your organization does not have one, communicate this statement to individuals within the nonprofit, and cultivate understanding of the statement among them.

2. Our mission will still be relevant in fifty to one hundred years.

    Donors who create planned gifts are investors in your long-term mission. If your nonprofit does not have a long time horizon, charitable gift planning is probably not for you.

3. We have a compelling need for charitable support to sustain our mission.

    If your nonprofit has no compelling need for charitable support, donors will not make planned gifts to support your mission. Focus your attention on why a nonprofit doesn't need charitable support first. If you can develop areas for charitable support, you can then establish an annual giving program followed by a gift planning effort.

Gift Planning Works Best When Your Organization Has a Long Time Horizon

I have done *pro bono* work for several churches that often receive bequests and want to encourage additional gifts. Their mission is clear and their standings in the community are well established. One is more than two hundred years old, with its first building having been burned by native Americans and its second structure having been burned by the British as part of the last battle of the American Revolution. Another is more than one hundred years old. In both cases, their constituents know and expect the organizations to be around for years to come, and they want to contribute to sustaining their growth.

—Robert

 stories from the real world

---

Compelling Need? *Not!*

I was asked by a marketing consultant to assist her in developing a gift planning strategy for a large membership organization. When we queried about the level of board support and annual gifts from the members, we were told that the board and membership considered their dues to be their support. Further discussion revealed that the organization owned its building outright, had no debt, had a very large endowment that more than covered its operating expenses, and had no plans for expansion or use for additional funds. We then asked why they wanted to pursue gift planning at this time. They explained, "We do not want to leave any money on the table that we could get from our members before they die."

—Brian

 stories from the real world

4. We have an effective strategic plan to implement our mission.

   Even nonprofits with well-articulated mission statements and cases will not garner support without also sharing strategic plans to illustrate to supporters how they will get there. The core priorities of a strategic plan not only guide thinking, but they also encourage donors to support those priorities. As the New Philanthropists (those born between 1946 and the present) set up their legacies, they will restrict those gifts. Best that your nonprofit has a strategic plan so that the gift restrictions are to your priority areas.

5. Our staff and board leadership are interested in pursuing long-term support.

   Many organizations are so caught up in raising money for the here and now that they lose sight of the long-term goal. If your board or staff leadership are among those who say we have to raise money for right now and cannot think about the future, you need to show them the elements of your internal case explaining why you have chosen to pursue charitable gift planning at this time.

6. We are financially stable.

   Donors want to support successful organizations. If your nonprofit doesn't look stable or successful, donors will seek others that do. Most donors will not make long-term investments through planned gifts in organizations that may not be around to use the planned gifts or might mismanage them.

7. We pursue endowments to ensure our long-term future.

   Endowments serve two key purposes for nonprofits. First, they pay for programs and expenses that the nonprofit will always pursue. Second, they allow the nonprofit to launch new initiatives it cannot afford from its operating budget. Every nonprofit has these two needs. If the board is not ready to raise money in this way, it is probably not the right time to pursue gift planning.

That's All, Folks

When we think of loyal donors, I can't think of a more important group than the board of any organization. Without its long-term support—both philosophically and financially—it will be next to impossible to lay the groundwork for a strong gift planning program to ensure the future. If you do your job well, you will help your donors leave a legacy that will help your organization endure. Without a gift planning program, it is possible that the board will be managing toward its own demise. The tombstone of Mel Blanc, the famous voice of Bugs Bunny and Porky Pig, reads "That's all, folks."

—Robert

observation

To Be Successful, Be Successful

I work with the Community Foundation of Herkimer and Oneida Counties, which offers charitable gift annuities to benefit area nonprofits. A donor to one of those nonprofits shared with me recently that she would never set up a gift annuity with the local nonprofit because she wasn't confident in its ability to manage it. She instead plans to set up a gift annuity through the Community Foundation, which has more assets.

—Brian

 stories from the real world

8. We regularly garner support from individuals.

Upon hearing about charitable gift planning, many nonprofits want to get started right away. Unfortunately, you do not just launch a gift planning program today. You start by putting in place several key pieces. One of those pieces is an individual gifts program. If you do not garner support from individuals, you cannot ask individuals to consider planned gifts.

9. We have a group of loyal donors who have supported us in the recent past.

Gift planning prospects are your loyal supporters, those who have invested in the cause year after year, regardless of amount. Without a pool of these prospects, it is impossible to know who to ask to consider a planned gift. If your program does not have annual supporters, start first with an annual giving program. Once you develop loyalty in that group, you can then pursue those individuals for planned gifts.

10. We have one hour per week for the next year to invest in gift planning.

Starting a charitable gift planning program takes time. You need to have the ability to invest a little time each week to build your program. But you'll see amazing results with just this modest investment if you make the commitment. You need to do the same if you want to be successful.

Legs of the Stool—Infrastructure, Prospect Interaction, and Marketing

The questionnaire has probably revealed strengths and weaknesses in your nonprofit, particularly as you approach launching a gift planning program. What you do with that information will determine whether your program succeeds or fails. Virtually every nonprofit that has ever asked us for assistance in building a gift planning program wants to jump right to the end. They ask for gift annuities,

---

Planned Gifts = Endowment = Mission

Several years ago, I met with the head of a large regional food bank to discuss starting a gift planning program. She told me that her organization needed every dollar it could find to feed the hungry in her service area today and that planned gifts were nice but not really helpful. I asked her how she would know when she had succeeded in meeting her organization's mission. She responded that once she had enough resources to know that she could provide for all of the hungry in her service area on any given day, the organization would have reached its goal. To which I responded: "Sounds like you need an endowment. How else can you be sure to have the resources needed to buy the food to feed the hungry every day?" When she thought about that for a while and realized that planned gifts are the best way to build endowments, she agreed to start a more robust gift planning effort.

—Brian

 stories from the real world

---

The Right Tool for the Right Job

British merchant Peter Durand first canned food in 1810, but the can opener wasn't invented until forty-eight years later by Ezra J. Warner. How many of us keep a hammer and chisel in our kitchen? That was what was used for nearly fifty years. While it opened the cans, it wasn't easy, and we can all agree that it is not the preferred method. Preparing for our gift planning program with the right tools in place is the preferred method.

 food for thought

complex assets, and fully integrated solutions right from the start. These are *stage two* and *stage three* tools. But if you do not build your program on a solid foundation—a three-legged stool made up of strong infrastructure, prospect interaction, and donor-focused marketing on a moves management platform— your program will not be sustainable. In **Parts Two**, **Three**, and **Four**, we discuss how you can build these key elements for your charitable gift planning program.

To Recap

◆ Before you embark on starting a gift planning program, ensure that your nonprofit is ready.

◆ Gift planning requires a mission suited to long-term support, an effective case, a strategic plan, engaged leaders, loyal supporters, and sufficient time and resources to pursue the program.

◆ If you are not ready, put your nonprofit in order first.

◆ Do not jump to the end. Build a sound program on a solid foundation with appropriate infrastructure, prospect interaction, and marketing.

Part Two

Infrastructure

You're on your way. Your organization understands the importance of gift planning to its mission and has a case. You've reviewed your overall operation and you are ready to pursue it. The next step is to build the infrastructure that will support your gift planning program.

We say it several times throughout the book, but it bears repeating—most gift planning programs fail because they are not committed long term. They never put in place the core elements of a strong, sustainable program. Instead they "jump to the end" and offer complex gift planning tools without having the proper infrastructure and program plan to support it. Over time, the program loses momentum or other priorities take its place, and the nonprofit stops actively pursuing it. Sound familiar? We've seen it happen over and over.

You've already taken the first step to avoid this happening to your nonprofit by writing the internal case. You need to build the key elements of your infrastructure to ensure success. **Part Two** discusses how you can create a culture of donor-focused gift planning for your organization, the unique rules of ethics that guide charitable gift planning, and the roles of staff, board, volunteers, professional advisors, and consultants in helping build your program.

Chapter Three

Culture of Donor-focused Gift Planning

In This Chapter

···➔ Creating a culture of donor-focused gift planning for your organization

···➔ Laying the foundation for gift planning

···➔ Ethics

···➔ Know how to use your resources

Gift planning is not an activity pursued by one or two employees or volunteers; it is part of your organizational culture and strategic planning. To be successful, it starts with a strong culture of philanthropy.

A culture of philanthropy is hard to spot, but you know it when you see it. It's a feeling you get when you are involved. Whether you are a member of the program or development staff, a board member or donor, you know it through conversations. Everyone plays a part, and all contribute or detract. Excellent program encourages it, strong leadership guides it, engaged board members and volunteers are proud of it, and gift planning officers and other fundraisers cultivate it.

A culture of philanthropy, defined as a culture that synergistically motivates a giving response and investment from those who can relate to the organization's mission and worthiness, should be the goal of every nonprofit organization. It is the outcome from having a donor-focused fundraising program that not only cultivates giving but also practices stewardship. A program that enhances the mission and allows all to take pride in the part they play.

For a nonprofit organization to bring vision into reality, its staff, volunteers, and donors must take action first and lead by example, demonstrating their own commitment. The commitment is the basis for a culture of philanthropy. It is a platform from which the organization can ask its prospects to join in its efforts, but before you can talk to others, those closest to the mission must be on board.

As we'll discuss in the next chapter, the leader of the organization sets the course and culture of the nonprofit. To create a strong culture of philanthropy and ultimately of donor-focused gift planning, the CEO must work with the board to create a long-term strategic plan that can be at least partially funded through philanthropy. The CEO must then commit the organization, from the lowest-level employees to the wealthiest board members, to treating all they engage on behalf of the nonprofit as potentially seven-figure donors.

Creating a Culture of Donor-focused Gift Planning for Your Organization

As Jim Collins wrote in his book *From Good to Great,* leaders must go first. The culture of a company is the behavior of its leaders. Leaders get the behavior they exhibit and tolerate. So to change the culture of an organization, change the behavior of its leaders.

To build a gift planning program that fits with your unique set of donors and mission, your organization needs to create a donor-focused organizational culture, draft an internal case for gift planning, build or add to the existing individual gifts infrastructure, including annual gifts, major gifts, principal gifts, and gift planning, and finally engage staff and volunteer leadership in the creation of the program.

Culture comes from the Latin root *cultura,* which literally means cultivation. Creating a culture requires cultivating shared attitudes, values, goals, and practices that people in the organization, especially donors, live and feel.

Establish a Mindset

We all strive to practice good stewardship with our donors, but the same care in saying thanks to our supporters can go a long way with those who give in other ways. Those who provide their time and talent to your mission can appreciate our thanks as well. And as the change agents in your organization, their continued courtesy goes a long way toward building a culture of philanthropy. It is easy to encourage philanthropy among your development team and your board and volunteers, but to get those who haven't considered philanthropy to perhaps make their own gifts and to certainly support the idea of being user-friendly to donors they meet? That is challenging. But when it happens, you have gone a long way toward establishing a mindset that everyone buys into and supports.

observation

The Platinum Rule of Fundraising

Organizations with a true culture of philanthropy treat everyone like top-level prospects. This requires training your entire team of staff, volunteers, board members, and others who are in contact with the public to follow the platinum rule of fundraising: treat others as they want to be treated. For example, this means that people who answer the phones need to be polite and helpful. If they cannot solve a problem, they should not transfer callers to another line and hope it gets resolved. They should stay on the line with the callers until they connect with a live person who can solve the problem.

If everyone affiliated with your organization treats all they interact with on your behalf like they can give a million, millions will follow.

practical tip

Laying the Foundation for Gift Planning

Each nonprofit seeking to build a gift planning program should have previously developed a solid mission, a driving vision, a positioning statement, a strategic plan, and a case statement that clearly articulate the purpose of the nonprofit's existence, the plan to achieve its mission, and the case for why it is important.

> ### A Solid Foundation: Where It All Begins
>
> In his book *Top Performance*, Zig Ziglar said, "Your foundation determines how successful you will be." It all begins with a solid foundation.
>
> **" "**

If your organization is weak in these areas, start by working with your leadership to create a vision of the organization's direction, enhance familiarity with your activities, and create an understanding of how those activities relate to the mission and serve the greater community.

The long-term vision for the organization in conjunction with the organization's mission should be reflected in a strategic plan. This plan guides you, your staff, and your volunteers as you work toward annual goals that steadily grow year over year. A strategic plan is an organization's blueprint for carrying out its mission statement. It is initiated, implemented, and periodically reviewed by you and your board.

A strategic plan, which typically covers three to five years, is a prerequisite for establishing a general individual gifts fund development plan and, subsequently, your gift planning program. You simply cannot live without it. It identifies institutional priorities, plots a course for achieving goals and objectives, lays out performance assessments, and provides for midcourse corrections. The planning process should involve the advancement team and key volunteers, including board members and even major donors. These key constituents have a vested interest in the organization and should show a level of responsibility that causes their later support. This is exactly the reason to involve board members and donors. Their buy-in today should lead to their financial support tomorrow. Developing a strategic plan is one of the very first recommendations we make to most organizations.

Your mission and strategic plan drive your *external* case statement. In **Part One**, we discuss your *internal* case for gift planning, which keeps your staff and board engaged in gift planning for the long term. The *external* case has a different role: expressing potential reasons why the prospective donors might want to contribute to the advancement of the cause. It describes your goals and objectives and explains the role of philanthropy in achieving those goals. It also covers the programs and services provided. There is one large case for the organization from which smaller individual case statements are developed for various constituencies or programs.

With the mission and vision statements, a strategic plan, and a case statement in place, you have built a culture supportive of gift planning and can begin to build the balance of your infrastructure.

Ethics

Before you jump right into practice, it is worthwhile to review the rules of gift planning ethics. Gift planning is a specialized field of endeavor. Likely for the first time, you and your nonprofit are dealing with prospects in ways that provide you with access to personal and financial information that you may not have been privy to in past gift discussions. Due to the sensitivity of this information, it is important to recognize the ethical rules and regulations that may apply to your work.

Relationships are based on trust, and at the core of that trust is how we act with character and integrity. Our ethics guide our actions and maintain the trust that people place in us as fundraisers.

When gift planning emerged as a profession, there were no standards of ethics. While many of the professionals involved in gift planning (attorneys, accountants, financial advisors, etc.) were subject to *their own* ethical standards, the field of gift planning itself had none. In 1991, the National Committee on Planned Giving (now the Partnership for Philanthropic Planning) adopted the first set of *Model Standards of Practice for the Charitable Gift Planner*. These standards provide the groundwork for responsible gift planning by charities and professional advisors. We strongly encourage you to download the current version of the Model Standards of Practice for the Charitable Gift Planner at *pppnet.org*.

The standards remind us that at the heart of every planned gift is the charitable motivation of the donor. Without charitable intent, a planned gift makes little sense, as there are more attractive commercially available financial alternatives to virtually every planned gift structure. The model standards:

> **Always Put the Donors First**
>
> Do you have the integrity to say *no* to a gift? My organization has been stewarding for several years a million-dollar donor and his wife. They recently asked about supporting a new project where their names would adorn a building. We offered three options to which they responded, "We could use the cash from our second-to-die policy to cover the pledge for the first year." They were correct, but I had to remind them that they and their financial planner had designated that policy for their son to pay the estate taxes upon their passing and we didn't want to negatively impact that plan. I reiterated that we would work together to find a solution that integrated with their overall financial and estate plan. They appreciated our stance to put them and their family first so our discussion continues....
>
> —Robert

 **stories from the real world**

- ◆ suggest that donors should be made aware of the tax implications of their planned gifts;

- ◆ call for full disclosure of representation and compensation so that donors know who represents who and how charitable representatives and professional advisors are compensated;

- ◆ prohibit the payment of commissions on charitable gifts in all cases; and

- ◆ call on charitable representatives to be competent and professional.

Be especially careful if you have access to a donor's financial and personal information. You have this information not to satisfy your curiosity or the curiosity of your peers but to help the donor create a meaningful gift plan. All personal and financial information should be in your confidential database, with access granted only to those who need it. Protecting the privacy of each donor's information will go a long way toward building the trust required to facilitate meaningful planned gifts.

If you follow all of the steps outlined in *Getting Started in Charitable Gift Planning* and the *Resource Book*, you will know enough to successfully offer basic bequests, retirement plan beneficiary designations, and life insurance policy beneficiary designations to your donors without worry or concern. But if you start to move into more complex gifts, such as those involving gift annuities, charitable trusts, lead trusts, private foundations, or complex assets, you may need more training or professional guidance.

In fact, the model standards suggest when you start to work on more complex gifts that you call a professional advisor and that you always suggest to donors that they contact their own advisors before making planned gifts.

Ultimately, the model standards are to ensure the public trust. If charities do not regulate themselves, carrying themselves with fairness, honesty, integrity, and openness, then they betray the people they were created to serve. Without self-regulation, the government is likely to make the charitable giving process far more difficult or eliminate charitable giving incentives all together in favor of government-run programs.

You Do Not Need to Be a Technical Expert—Gift Planning Is Easy

Gift planning has long been thought of as one of the mysterious arts of fundraising. Those who are skilled in this area were thought to be wizards with taxes and estate planning. They talked about fancy things and used terminology that resembled another language. Terms like CRATs and CRUTs, CLATs and CLUTs, and CGAs and PIFs all sound very strange indeed, but we'll decipher this alphabet soup in **Part One** of the resource book. Gift planning is not, in fact, about the technical tools or complex plans. It is about relationship building. If you build relationships with people close to your mission and ask them for long-term support, your program will be successful. We'll share the resources that will allow you to work to support your donors without worrying about the technical jargon. Gift planning is easy.

Know How to Use Your Resources— Renting versus Owning Expertise

We outline many steps that should be taken to build your own gift planning program, but you may at some point say, "This is great, but we have limited development staff" or "I'm only one person; how can I do all of this?" That could very well be the case. You have options. You can enlist volunteers to assist with tasks they can handle. You can invest in programs, such as Planned Giving in a Box and Planned Giving Essentials, to assist you in this process.

Partnering with Allied Professionals

Partnering can help you reach your goals. While I have a background in financial planning, and while I held insurance licenses and had SEC registrations, I no longer am a financial representative. During my time with the American Cancer Society, I learned of the value of using its National Professional Advisor Network to build relationships with professionals who could assist me in my work with prospects. On many occasions, a prospect was able to complete a gift because of their help. Whether you create a philanthropic planning council or a professional advisors network to support your organization, consider how attorneys, accountants, financial planners, and other professionals can help you in your work. In my experience, they are a tremendous resource!

—Robert

 stories from the real world

If you want even more help, you can hire a consultant to help build your program. There are many full-service consulting firms, but from what we have learned, getting a firm that specializes in gift planning can be money well spent. These firms know what you are trying to do and have done it many times. They bring their knowledge and experience to your doorstep and can also represent you with your donors to close gifts. When you consider the cost of a part-time consultant who spends a day a week in your office as opposed to a full-time development officer who would need a salary plus benefits, the net value is a great option to reach your goals.

Keep in mind that you do not have to spend a significant amount of money for this expertise. In days past, many nonprofits hired full-time gift planning officers who spent most of their days not doing gift planning. In this day and age, that kind of expenditure is not justified. Instead, you can put a professional advisor with strong gift planning background, or a gift planning consultant, on retainer and have the expertise available when you need it, without paying for it all the time. This is renting the expertise rather than owning it.

To Recap

◆ A culture of philanthropy should be the goal for every organization.

◆ To build a gift planning culture, an organization needs to create a donor-focused organizational culture.

◆ Practicing good ethics should be a core value of your organization. It is imperative to establishing public trust.

◆ Gift planning is easy. You do not have to be a technical expert. You just need to know how to use your resources.

◆ Consider using consultants to fill in the gaps on your development team. Several good options exist, and it allows you to have the program that you want and your organization needs without hiring additional full-time staff.

Chapter Four

Your Role in Gift Planning

In This Chapter

···→ Where do you fit in the puzzle?

···→ Each member of the team has a role to play

···→ Working with volunteers

···→ Collaboration with your colleagues

Everyone affiliated with your nonprofit has a role in the fundraising effort, and everyone affiliated with the fundraising effort has a role in gift planning. Whether you are the CEO, top-level executive, gift planner, development officer, or volunteer, you are responsible for helping create and enhance your gift planning program. And depending upon the size and scope of your staff, that role can differ from organization to organization.

Where Do You Fit in the Puzzle?

For years (and even to this day), we came across organizations that hired development directors and said, "Okay, now go raise money." The director was usually gone within six months to a year, having made very little progress. The organization would blame the fundraiser, and the fundraiser would blame the organization. Unfortunately, there is usually plenty of blame to go around. It pointed to the lack of a culture of philanthropy. Fundraising is everyone's job. If the culture of the organization is not set up that way, it makes it almost impossible for a fundraiser to be successful.

Similarly, gift planning does not operate in a vacuum. In many ways, it is a service provided by one or more people in the organization to those responsible for fundraising. If those responsible do not see themselves as service providers, it makes it very difficult to move the program forward. Similarly, if the staff and volunteers see gift planning as "someone else's job," then the program will languish. The person responsible for gift planning needs to engage the rest of the staff and volunteers, and the staff and volunteers need to look for opportunities to introduce gift planning ideas with prospects. When

> ### Size Matters
>
> Although it may seem that larger nonprofits have significant advantages in gift planning, this is not always true. We have worked with several large research universities to re-imagine their gift planning programs. Due to the existing transactional, institution-focused culture, it has often proved impossible to fully implement a donor-focused model, particularly for the highest-level prospects, where gift and philanthropic planning could have the most impact. The smaller organizations, with less entrenched bureaucracy, tend to be more open to change and are able to more readily evolve their culture, resulting in more planned gifts. Do not let your size deter you from embracing a donor-focused gift planning effort.
>
>  **stories from the real world**

configured in this way, gift planning programs add tremendous value, sometimes reaching 40 percent of the total gifts raised from individuals.

President/CEO/Executive Director

As the leader of the organization, the president/CEO/executive director (CEO) sets the course and culture of the nonprofit. If there is to be a strong culture of philanthropy and ultimately of donor-focused gift planning, it has to start from the top. The CEO works with the board to develop the vision, strategy, and strategic planning to support the mission of the organization. If the strategic plan lacks long-term vision, it will be nearly impossible to start an effective gift planning program. If the board is not prepared by the CEO to assist with community outreach and fundraising using its understanding of the community and the market for the nonprofit, the fundraising and gift planning programs will fail.

In larger organizations, the CEO oversees the staff and hires the chief development officer (CDO), ideally a person who shares the CEO's vision for the organization. With a CDO in place, the CEO has a supportive role, with the board, staff, volunteers, and donors participating in the cultivation, solicitation, and stewardship of top-level prospects. Most major donors will want to talk to the CEO when asked to support an organization. They will want to hear from the nonprofit's leader about the mission and vision.

When asked by the development team, the CEO must be willing to go on cultivation and solicitation calls. The CEO's involvement can be the difference between a "yes" and a "no." Other than friends or peers who have already made their own gifts and then asked the prospect to join them in making a gift, the CEO is the best one to make an ask to your highest-level prospect. When having a stewardship event with your legacy society, the CEO is the ideal person to give an update to those gift planning donors.

The most successful CEOs understand the fundraising process. In our experience, they make personal annual leadership gifts, major gifts when appropriate, and planned gifts.

In smaller nonprofits, the CEO may also be the CDO. In fact, for the vast majority of nonprofits in the United States with paid staff, this is likely the case. For the CEO wearing many hats, gift planning often is seen as the last place to spend time. However, when you consider that gift planning can produce up to 40 percent of

> ### Leadership is...
>
> *Leadership is the art of getting someone else to do something that you want done because he wants to do it.*
>
> —President Dwight D. Eisenhower, 34th president of the United States and five-star general in the US Army serving as Supreme Commander of the Allied Forces in Europe during World War II
>
> " "

individual gifts revenue and that planned gifts typically result in endowments, which produce permanent funding streams, the gift planning hat must be put on by the small nonprofit CEO.

The good news is that 80 percent of all gift planning revenue comes from naming your nonprofit as the beneficiary of a will, retirement plan, life insurance policy, donor-advised fund, payable-on-death account, or transfer-on-death asset. By learning about these easy-to-execute planned gifts that cost your prospects nothing today, the small nonprofit CEO can be amazingly effective in gift planning with little to no training or expertise. If you need help beyond this book in building such a program, Planned Giving in a Box is designed to help you do just this. For more information, visit *plannedgivinginabox.com.*

What New Philanthropists Want to Know

New Philanthropists are investing in your organization. They want to understand, prior to making their commitment, that they are making a sound investment—one that will reap rewards from their gifts.

Chief Development Officer/Vice President of Development/Director of Development

The CEO chooses who will lead the development program of the organization. In larger organizations, this is usually a chief development officer or vice president of development, whereas in smaller organizations, it can be a director of development (if it is not the CEO). The people in these roles (CDOs) should be on the CEO's executive team. This is important for the standing of the development office in the organization as well as the importance of the office in the eyes of the community. The CDO should report directly to the CEO as a vital relationship in the organization and have direct board contact.

The CDO creates the fundraising strategy in coordination with the strategic plan and then supervises the success of the strategy according to performance metrics, as discussed in the next chapter. The CDO is responsible for crafting the case for support and identifying prospects most likely to invest in the cause.

In a larger nonprofit, the CDO will organize and oversee the activities involving the CEO and select board members when it comes to cultivation, solicitation, and stewardship of donors. The CDO will also hire and supervise a staff of development professionals, which could include a director for each individual gifts area: annual giving, major giving, principal giving, and gift planning. In turn, there would be development officers reporting to the directors who do most of the relationship building with donors in their respective portfolios. Collectively, the CDO will want to maintain and grow the donor pool for the organization where all four main program areas are supporting the mission.

The CDO will ensure that gift reports, gift agreements, and gift policies are maintained. The CDO will measure performance objectives and

Lunch and Learns

I have found it helpful to educate those around me in the concepts and tools of charitable gift planning. Whether it was major gift or development officers, or professional advisors, I have used "Lunch & Learns" sessions to increase the level of knowledge for those who can assist me in my work. By inviting colleagues who can benefit from a presentation or discussion on an interesting gift case to join you for lunch in a conference room, you have a chance to not only position yourself as an expert, but you also open up lines of communication and referrals.

—Robert

will benchmark performance for comparison against organizational peers in the sector.

In the gift planning context, the CDO is responsible for setting up a team environment. While the CEO sets the culture of philanthropy, the CDO puts it into play. The most successful gift planning programs can be found in organizations where the CDO has directed that all major and principal gift relationships include the director of gift planning. Without this team-based directive, many major and principal gifts will not be optimized for the donor or the nonprofit, resulting in smaller gift totals.

> **Do You Have a Trained Gift Planner on Staff?**
>
> If you have a trained gift planner on your staff, put that person to the highest and best use: working with prospects. Hire other staff to ensure that the gift planning infrastructure and marketing are in place and effective.
>
> **!** important

For the smaller nonprofit with a CEO and a CDO, the CDO will also be the primary gift planning officer. Just as we suggested when the CEO plays this role, the CDO should focus on the simple planned gifts since they are the source of the majority of the dollars. Over time, the CDO will learn about more complex gift plans as particular donor situations require. Remember, you can always rent the expertise you do not own.

Director of Gift Planning

In large organizations, the director of gift planning (DGP) oversees all three legs of the gift planning program: infrastructure, prospect interaction, and marketing gift planning. To understand the role of a DGP, read each chapter in this book and follow the steps. The director of gift planning will provide a plan and strategy to identify, cultivate, solicit, and steward donors and prospects toward planned gifts.

Normally, a DGP will have some additional members on the gift planning team to help implement marketing strategies and build the infrastructure. We consistently counsel nonprofits to put gift planners to their highest and best use: working with prospects. When gift planners work without administrative support or without help in marketing and infrastructure, it limits their ability to collaborate with other fundraisers, build relationships, and facilitate planned gifts from your prospects. In the next chapter, we illustrate the reduced benchmarks for gift planners who also have other duties.

> **We Created Partnerships with Major and Principal Gift Officers**
>
> When I arrived at the University of Pennsylvania, we had a reactive gift planning shop that provided services when needed. We moved to change that, including offering partnerships with major and principal gift officers. By the time I left Penn, our complex outright gifts (real estate, collectibles, business interests, etc.) outpaced our life-income gifts for the first time since the university started keeping those records. The partnerships with major and principal gift officers produced those gifts, meeting both donor needs and institutional goals.
>
> —Brian
>
>  **stories from the real world**

When working with prospects, the DGP has two constituencies—an internal constituency of other fundraisers in the organization and an outside constituency made up of volunteers, board members, professional advisors, and prospects. In **Parts Two** and **Three**, we discuss how to work collaboratively with external audiences. Internally, the DGP must constantly work to partner with other fundraisers to help build donor-focused strategies for prospects. This often involves joint visits to bring those relationships along, collaboration with the prospects' professional advisors, and finding creative solutions to meet personal planning objectives. Frequently this is done behind the scenes, while the primary fundraiser is front and center. These partnerships, particularly for principal and major gift prospects, often result in the largest gifts that charities receive. But building that trust takes time. Major and principal gift officers are often concerned that by bringing a gift planner to the table, a major gift could be turned into a planned gift. It is important for you to work with your major and principal gift officers to help them reach their goals while also working to reach the goals of the nonprofit and the donor.

At one time, director of gift planning was seen as an up-and-coming field. Most large and medium-sized shops were looking to add gift planning specialists to their staff, and "in-the-know" fundraisers realized that they could make more money as gift planning specialists than as development officers. As a result, the Partnership for Philanthropic Planning, the national organization of gift planners, grew to over eleven thousand members at its peak. It now has fewer than six thousand members. In many cases, the duties of the director of gift planning have been split among major gift officers and other development officers to handle in a hybrid role.

Years ago, when it was called deferred giving, CDOs would hire technicians who were knowledgeable about life-income vehicles and computing deductions but lacked the relationship-building skills that would truly serve them as they worked with their donors to meet their needs and exceed their expectations. You can always get technical support or advice, but nothing can take the place of establishing a relationship with a donor to your organization. Ultimately, this is why these new models can and should work. All fundraisers are trained in relationship building and basic gift planning, and you rent expertise for complex gifts when you need it.

For smaller shops, you likely do not have a gift planning specialist at all. For you, it is vitally important to have resources available when anything beyond a basic beneficiary designation is proposed or appears to warrant discussion. Be sure to have a gift planning consultant or attorney knowledgeable in gift planning on retainer for these situations.

Development Officers

If your organization has a CEO, CDO, and one or more development officers, you are fortunate. Many nonprofits do not elect to make this level of investment in fundraising. But with multiple people in the department and still no gift planning specialist,

> **Expertise in Identifying a Prospect Is Vital**
>
> Every fundraiser today should be looking to learn about all four areas of development so as to be well versed in support of donors. While you may still seek gift planning expertise to assist with a donor, your practical knowledge in identifying a prospect who may be interested in gift planning is vital in your role. Training programs from AFP (*afpnet.org*) and PPP (*pppnet.org*) are excellent resources to help you keep up to date.
>
>

development officers need to be trained and kept updated on gift planning processes and tools to take advantage of opportunities that may arise unexpectedly with donors. Major gift donors usually make a series of escalating gifts during their lifetimes, which often include planned gifts. Development officers need to be capable of identifying gift planning opportunities and facilitating major and planned gifts. Building your knowledge in gift planning can prepare you to handle whatever may appear in the process of donor cultivation.

A Charitable Gift Annuity vs. a Certificate of Deposit

Janis is an active volunteer who is a terrific ambassador in the community. After several years of loyal service and annual support, she wanted to consider an alternative to the poor interest rate offered by her bank for her certificate of deposit. She inquired about a charitable gift annuity, as she had heard me present this option to the ladies auxiliary at the hospital. Now that she has made her first planned gift, she has told me that she not only plans to do others but regularly talks with her friends about it.

—Robert

stories from the real world

Volunteers

Volunteers are often the lifeblood of fundraising programs, particularly to leverage the resources of a smaller organization. But regardless of your size, volunteers are an integral part of the process, not only as donors but as engaged members in the overall development program. As peers, they can introduce and refer new prospects to the organization. Their active participation, while providing a stewardship experience, also justifies how the organization is perceived in the community and how others see their actions and leadership by example.

In the gift planning context, volunteers often sway their peers to consider planned gifts. They have a faith and trust in each other that they may not have in your organization or your capacity to share information about gift planning. Throughout **Parts One**, **Two**, and **Three**, we have identified opportunities to engage volunteers in your process.

Collaboration with Your Colleagues

It isn't enough to know what your role is as it relates to gift planning. As a strong nonprofit professional, you will want to know how you can mesh with your colleagues to make the rest of the team better. A donor-focused, service-based program will build lasting relationships with the donors of your organization. Maximizing the benefits of the donor's gift for both the donor and the organization is the right approach.

To Recap

◆ The CEO of the organization plays an integral role in the cultivation and solicitation of your best donors from the top tier of your prospect list.

◆ The CDO develops the strategy and plan for fundraising development and then oversees the activity for donor cultivation.

◆ Each member of the nonprofit team has a valuable role to make a gift planning program successful. If your organization has one, the director of gift planning develops the strategy and plan for gift planning activity.

Gift Planning in Independent Schools and Liberal Arts Colleges

Many independent schools and liberal arts colleges use a robust class volunteer program to promote planned gifts. They have a gift planning representative in each class and during the reunion cycle set goals for the percentage of each class that created a planned gift and that had the largest increase in gift planning participation. This creates wonderful class rivalries and significant peer-to-peer asks that result in planned gifts. One school has added a matching gift component to further entice participation. These schools tend to have much higher planned gift participation rates than similar schools without such programs.

stories from the real world

◆ Like with all of your development activities, recording your efforts in a donor cultivation software program will not only be helpful for your colleagues to follow activity but will also be vital to future members in the organization to see the history with a donor.

◆ In a donor-focused gift planning program, collaboration with your colleagues is directly related to the success that can be achieved. If all work together, with the needs of the donor as the common denominator, then your gift planning program will flourish.

◆ The fundraiser of today needs to know and be able to apply concepts from annual, major, and planned giving.

Chapter Five

Performance Goals

In This Chapter

···→ Performance goals for your organization

···→ Performance goals for individuals

···→ Measuring the success of your gift planning efforts

···→ Benchmarking

I n this day and age, it is impossible to build a program without performance goals, metrics, and benchmarking. Boards demand them, and when they are aligned with your strategic plan, they keep you on track. Gift planning requires performance goals for the organization, individual fundraisers, and overall success.

A performance metric is a measure of an organization's activities and performance. Performance metrics should support a range of organizational and donor needs. Strategic performance measures monitor the implementation and effectiveness of an organization's strategies, determine the gap between actual and targeted performance, and determine organizational effectiveness and operational efficiency. Like the compass and charts on a ship, performance metrics can help a charity's leadership steer the direction and plot the location of the organization as it continues on its journey.

Performance Goals for Your Organization

For an organization to measure success, leadership should create a strategy and plan for gift planning for fundraisers and volunteers. It should include goals and objectives as well as action plans that outline the specific steps and activities that will drive the desired results.

The plan should include components for all three segments of the prospects to be targeted—major and principal gifts prospects, donors with no major gift capacity, and everyone else—in the three core areas of donor interaction: marketing, stewardship, and program development.

Measuring the success of your gift planning program is difficult. Unlike annual giving with its schedule of mailings to certain numbers of prospects and then responses and dollar amounts for resulting gifts, or major giving in a capital campaign with a specific time frame and dollar goal, gift planning must be measured by activity. If you pursue gift planning regularly and consistently, dollar results will follow.

The activity involved in your gift planning program matches the strategy set by leadership and should be measured by performance metrics that are deemed important in your organization. Good gift planning performance measures:

◆ provide a way to see if your strategy is working;

◆ focus fundraisers' and volunteers' attention on what matters most to success;

◆ allow measurement of accomplishments, not just of the work that is performed;

◆ provide a common language for communication;

◆ are explicitly defined in terms of owner, unit of measure, collection frequency, data quality, expected value (targets), and thresholds;

◆ are valid, to ensure measurement of the right things; and

◆ are verifiable, to ensure data collection accuracy.

> ### Is Your Organization Great?
>
> *Good is the enemy of great. And that is one of the reasons that we have so little that becomes great. We don't have great schools, principally because we have good schools. We don't have great government, principally because we have good government. Few people attain great lives, precisely because it is easy to settle for a good life. The vast majority of companies never become great precisely because they become quite good—and that is their main problem.*
>
> —Jim Collins, author, *Good to Great: Why Some Companies Make the Leap . . . and Others Don't* (Harper Collins 2001)
>
> Do not let your gift planning program be good enough. With the right metrics, it can indeed be great.
>
>

These measures lead us to the following performance metrics for the gift planning program:

◆ Number of visits with gift planning prospects by type of visit (i.e., qualification, cultivation, solicitation, negotiation, and stewardship)

◆ Number of quality contacts with gift planning prospects (including those through your marketing program)

◆ Number of marketing responses (and to which specific marketing pieces)

◆ Number of professional advisor meetings

◆ Number of legacy society qualifying asks

◆ Number of collaborations with other gift officers, volunteers, and senior staff to discuss planned gifts

◆ Number, type, and amount of gift planning commitments

◆ Number, type, and amount of matured planned gifts

◆ Total marketing cost

◆ Total expenses

Once the plan is implemented, your nonprofit should evaluate its performance against the plan each month, at the end of each fiscal year, and over a ten-year window. By monitoring performance metrics for each area of the plan, adjustments can be made to drive success. Later in this chapter, we'll also discuss how benchmarking helps an organization understand where it is positioned relative to its peers in a specific sector.

Performance Goals for Individuals

In addition to tracking the performance for the program, metrics should be set to track the performance for individual fundraisers in all of the same areas except dollars raised. Dollar goals are often thought to be an important indicator of success, but they are often misunderstood and do not tell the whole story of an individual's activity. We recommend that you do not use them to measure performance but, instead, track them to compare results year over year. After all, a significant portion of the dollar results come from realized bequests and are received only if "the right people die" in a given time frame.

As many of the planned gifts that result from gift planning are delayed due to their testamentary nature, the use of difficult-to-value complex assets, or their long development cycle with the donor and their advisors, dollars raised are not a good representation of the work completed by the fundraiser.

One of the most important and often-overlooked metrics is collaboration. In the donor-focused model we suggest, many gift planning conversations are started by someone other than the gift planner—especially when an organization doesn't have a gift planner! If fundraisers, volunteers, and senior staff all collaborate on strategy and include gift planning suggestions at the appropriate time, your nonprofit will maximize philanthropy from your donors. By measuring collaboration, and emphasizing its importance, you will dramatically improve your results and your numbers of satisfied donors.

While dollar goals should not be used to measure performance, you should have a consistent method to track gift results. To do so, we suggest that you use the three categories, set forth in the Partnership for Philanthropic Planning (PPP) counting standards (*http://bit.ly/pppguidelines*):

Measuring Performance

For an established gift planning officer, it is not unreasonable to expect $1 million in planned gifts annually, as it was when I worked for the American Cancer Society. Many factors can contribute to reaching or missing dollar goals. I was fortunate to be in the New York Metropolitan area as the director of planned giving for New Jersey, which is not only a more affluent area than much of the country, but it is also heavily populated and its residents are very aware of cancer as a health concern. Needless to say, it was never an issue to meet the minimum goal for planned gifts. And while I always surpassed the minimum dollar amount, it didn't really account for all my visits with professional advisors who regularly referred clients to me and to whom I was also able to refer business. The dollar amount also didn't give credit to the phone calls made, the cultivation and solicitation visits, the many meetings with volunteers to ask for referrals, etc. All of it supported my success.

—Robert

observation

◆ *Category A:* outright gifts. Gifts that are usable or will become usable for institutional purposes during the counting period, including cash from realized bequests, trust liquidations, life insurance and commercial annuity beneficiaries received, complex asset gifts, and securities.

◆ *Category B:* irrevocable deferred gifts. Gifts committed during the reporting period but likely usable by the organization only at some point after the end of the period, including charitable remainder trusts, charitable gift annuities, pooled-income funds, and other split-interest gifts.

◆ *Category C:* revocable deferred gifts. Gifts solicited and committed during the reporting period but for which the donor retains the right to change the commitment and/or beneficiary, including beneficiary designations on wills, living trusts, life insurance policies, retirement plans, donor-advised funds, payable-on-death accounts, and transfer-on-death assets.

> ### The Problem with Assigning Dollar Goals to Fundraisers
>
> Assigning dollar goals to fundraisers seems so old fashioned, so limiting, so inappropriate, so out of step with what really matters. It doesn't adequately take into account the economy, or the effect that other parts of the organization can have on fund development—for example, the quality of the program and the cultivation, solicitation, and stewardship process with donors.
>
>
> **important**

A sample gift-counting summary, based on the PPP standards, can be found in Chapter Six of the *Resource Book.*

Measuring the Success of Your Gift Planning Efforts

It is typical that the time it takes to cultivate and solicit a planned gift will stretch beyond the normal cycle of a fiscal year. You need to measure activity each year but also over five-year cycles to truly evaluate the performance of your gift planning program. Single snapshots rarely tell the whole story. In **Part Three** of the *Resource Book,* we offer charts to track your performance metrics currently and over time.

> ### The Nobility of Gift Planning
>
> *It takes a noble person to plant a tree that will one day provide shade for those whom he or she may never meet.*
>
> —Anonymous
>
> " "

Many of the planned gifts that you develop will come to fruition years after you have served the organization you now represent. Similarly, many of the realized bequests that mature during your tenure with the organization may be the result of those who came before you. We are seeing this in real life. Robert currently leads the gift planning program at a nonprofit for which Brian set up the gift planning program fifteen years ago. It seems that almost every month, Robert shares a story with Brian about a recently deceased donor who Brian and later Robert had the opportunity to cultivate and steward. It is a powerful reminder of the long-term nature of our work.

Benchmarking

Benchmarking has been an important development in the evolution of fundraising. Professional associations like PPP and AFP, and then sector-specific associations like the Council for the Advancement and Support of Education (CASE) for higher education, the Association for Healthcare Philanthropy (AHP), and the Advisory Board (a national consulting and research firm) for health care, have all looked at benchmarks and provided sector-specific statistics. Yet, while it has been identified as a benefit, the nonprofit sector has not set its own industry-wide benchmarks.

To see where your organization stands against like organizations, benchmarking is a useful tool. First, determine why you want to benchmark and define your desired outcomes. You can then make a plan to gather your metrics and then select your benchmarking peers or partners. Finally, gather data from their metrics and compare and analyze the results. The information can be helpful to knowing how you are succeeding in relation to your niche in your sector.

In addition to the performance measurements that have been discussed, the number of bequests, charitable gift annuities, life insurance and commercial annuity beneficiaries, and charitable remainder trusts are all numbers that can be compared with other like organizations. As this sidebar illustrates, you can also look to your national association office for these statistics if your division is part of a larger organization.

Return on Philanthropic Investment

It is possible to benchmark the cost to raise a dollar, a measure of fundraising efficiency, and return on investment, a measure of fundraising effectiveness. To do so, you will need to track results over much longer periods of time, typically ten years in the gift planning context. Since fundraisers have an average tenure of sixteen months, these benchmarks measure organizational efficiency and effectiveness rather than individual performance.

> ### Benchmarking Among Divisions
>
> If you work for a national organization, it is interesting to benchmark performance amongst divisions. The Boy Scouts of America and the American Cancer Society do a terrific job in benchmarking performance at the local council level and division level, respectively, to compare the number of bequest commitments, realized bequests, and average size of realized bequests and then also the number of charitable gift annuities and average size of gift annuities. Not only is the information helpful, but since they also know information about the size of their local council or division, they can also compare performance relative to other like-size councils and divisions.
>
> —Robert
>
> **stories from the real world**

In recent years, concerns have been raised that cost to raise a dollar and return on investment are not good measures for nonprofits. Dan Pallotta, creator of the multiday charitable event industry, and Life is Good co-founder Bert Jacobs have both suggested that when you limit spending, you limit the ability of nonprofits to pursue really big ideas the way that businesses do. The result of these metrics, in their opinion, is a nonprofit sector that does not innovate or solve problems as quickly as it could. Should you elect to use these measures, keep their limitations in mind.

To be truly innovative, we suggest that you develop a new measure for your nonprofit called return on philanthropic investment (RPI). RPI measures your cost per dollar raised and your return on investment over ten-year periods, creating a long-term average that overcomes the analysis of individual budget years. Your organization would be able to effectively measure if its gift planning program is truly having the desired effect because the results of your long-term investments in the program would be counted against the fundraising expenses that likely led to those gifts. While this metric is not perfect, it is preferable to the current methodology, which focuses on individual fiscal years and never measures dollars spent on gift planning against actual dollars raised over time.

Are a Nonprofit's Peers *Really* Peers?

When working with clients, they almost always provide me with a list of organizations against which they "benchmark." These are the peer nonprofits against which they compare results. I consistently see two common mistakes. First, the organizations are not actually peers. They have a different donor base or appeal to a different sector. It is important that your peer nonprofits be actual peers. Second, they do not evaluate the quality of their peer group. Because I consult with multiple organizations in the same sector, I often find that the peer group includes nonprofits I work with directly. In many cases, even though the nonprofit appears to be a peer, it is not behaving like one. I recently had a school ask me to measure it against its peers. The school had a robust gift planning program that had been in place for years. Several schools in the peer group had placed no emphasis on gift planning at all. When I did the peer comparison, my client looked terrific on paper. But when I shared that the "peers" had made far less of an investment and had nearly two-thirds of the results of my client, they realized that maybe they were settling for "good enough" instead of trying to be great.

—Brian

To Recap

♦ A plan and strategy that outlines goals and objectives to measure performance will guide the organization toward success.

♦ Goals, objectives, and performance metrics for individuals that are based on activity around relationship building, donor cultivation, and stewardship will be most meaningful.

♦ Dollar goals can be misleading as a measurement of gift planning.

♦ Benchmarking can help compare your organization to other organizations in the sector.

♦ Return on philanthropic investment (RPI) is a more effective way to measure the true benefits of investing in your gift planning program.

Chapter Six

The Role of Your Board

In This Chapter

···→ Training your board members

···→ Setting expectations

···→ Board members as champions

···→ Every board member has to play a role

Most board members understand that fundraising is a core duty as well as a key priority for their organizations. Special events, annual giving, and sometimes major gifts are at the tops of their lists when discussing methods to raise revenue. Obviously, they will not want to leave out what should be a key component of their overall development plan—gift planning. As a person who is knowledgeable about its place in fundraising, the education of board members is an important job responsibility of every fundraiser.

It is not necessary to acquaint your board members with all of the tools and vehicles that encompass gift planning. Instead, use training to inform them about how gift planning can assist in the establishment or enhancement of long-term relationships with donors to the organization, how it can provide future funds, and how it encourages donors to think about assets as potential gifts can be the building blocks for further discussions. One important tool in the education process is a concise, donor-focused, internal case for gift planning.

Don't Underestimate the Value of Training Your Board Members

Do not be fooled into believing that your board members are sophisticated about gift planning. In 2012, I found myself talking to the largest donor of a nonprofit in the Midwest, who also happened to serve on its board. Until I mentioned it, he had no idea that he could donate real estate, which made up a significant portion of his personal wealth. He was able to make a much larger gift because I completed a simple board training.

—Brian

 stories from the real world

(A sample can be found in Chapter Six of the *Resource Book*.)

During the training and education process, you also have an opportunity to raise board member awareness of their own potential as gift planning prospects. Most board members are interested in one of the common benefits of gift planning, including:

- ◆ maximizing the inheritance of children or grandchildren

- ◆ increasing retirement income

- ◆ creating a more meaningful legacy

- ◆ providing for an elderly parent or loved one

- ◆ avoiding taxes

- ◆ diversifying assets

By including training for board members about gifts to meet personal planning objectives, you will get them thinking about their own gifts. Ideally, your board members will set up a planned gift for your organization prior to asking others to consider such a gift.

Did YOU Make a Planned Gift?

To get your board in the mood to make a planned gift, make one yourself! Both of us have done so with many organizations. It is easy to include your nonprofit as a beneficiary of some part of your life insurance policy or qualified retirement plan. And you'll find a much more receptive audience when you can say, "Won't you please join me in making a planned gift?"

Plant Seeds with Your Board Ahead of Time

While you live and breathe your nonprofit every day, many of your board members serve several organizations and are running businesses of their own. They do not have the time to think things through or read a lot of complex material.

To overcome this challenge, start to "plant seeds" well ahead of when you need the board to make decisions about gift planning. Suggest to members at a meeting that "sometime soon," we'll need to look at _____ (such as starting a gift annuity program). If you do this two or three times, you'll find that eventually the board members will approach you and say, "We really need to get to launching that gift annuity program." Instead of fighting to get the program approved, you'll be doing what the board has requested. It makes your job a lot easier.

Setting Expectations

With your board members educated, they are now in a position to understand and support gift planning. Let them know what is expected of them as it relates to their own giving and their roles as ambassadors of your organization's mission in the community. Roles should be defined, as should the extent of their legal responsibilities and board involvement with the gift planning program.

The board typically establishes investment policies and guidelines that include parameters for who makes investment decisions, where and how funds are to be invested, spending rate, and how gifts of stock are handled, to name a few. The board establishes policies regarding management, marketing, and promotion of the gift planning program. If the board members overseeing the delivery of programs and services of your nonprofit are not in agreement with the process of soliciting gifts, they will not be effective advocates for your fundraising efforts. They will determine what types of gift planning vehicles will be offered as well as a minimum amount to accept for each instrument. For example, most organizations use $10,000 as a minimum for charitable gift annuities.

Board Members as Champions

Board members should be ambassadors, sharing the organization's mission, values, and programs. After making their own gifts, board members should help identify and cultivate prospects and open doors for you to build relationships and solicit gifts. By making use of their networks, board members make the organization stronger and able to survive change. They should become the biggest advocates for your gift planning program.

When you consider that various studies indicate that 75 to 85 percent of the adults in the United States die without a *valid and current* will, it becomes clear that there is much work to do. When you factor in that, according to the *Chronicle of Philanthropy*, one out of four Americans is willing to consider a charitable bequest, the opportunity is there for your board members to open conversations and convert estate intentions into actual planned gifts.

Every Board Member Has to Play a Role

Many board members are not comfortable making an ask, particularly a gift planning ask. However, fundraising is one of the most important jobs for the board. Instead of forcing the issue, share with your board that everyone has to play a role, but not everyone has to play the *same* role. This allows board members to use their talents while not requiring that each "make the ask."

Noted major gift development expert, Karen Osborn, tells us that a culture of philanthropy exists when 100 percent of the board members give joyfully at a level commensurate with each one's ability; when all are informed and passionate ambassadors telling the story, introducing the institution to others, and gladly and freely sharing expertise and wisdom; and when all see philanthropy as an aspect of every committee's role.

> ### Never Underestimate the Power of a Board Member as a Champion of Your Program
>
> Never underestimate the power of a board member as a champion for your gift planning program. One of my community foundation clients brought me in to build a proactive development program, including a gift annuity program. The chair of the Marketing and Development Committee was eager to get the gift annuity program started because she herself wanted to establish a gift annuity for the benefit of the organization. By the time we completed the various steps, it was year-end, but she was the first donor in the door with a six-figure gift annuity. She brought with her another six-figure gift annuitant. Five months later, a $1 million gift annuity came in the door.
>
> At the same time, she has become a champion of the community foundation, offering gift annuities on behalf of other charities in the area that are not financially able to take on this responsibility. At the time of this writing, there are six area charities eager to participate, each with multiple gift annuitants in the wings. One champion on your board can be a huge resource and help attract significant planned gifts.
>
> —Brian
>
>  stories from the real world

In addition to referrals to prospects, you can also gain introductions to professional advisors through board members. Whether they are trust officers, estate or tax attorneys, accountants, insurance professionals, investment advisors, financial planners, bankers, funeral directors, or real estate brokers, professional advisors can be strong partners in developing your gift planning program. Involving board members in cultivation activities with advisors can also further educate them about the process of gift planning.

To Recap

◆ Fundraising is a core duty for each board member as well as a key priority for every organization.

◆ While they don't need to understand all of the tools of gift planning, every board member can assist in identifying gift planning opportunities.

◆ Educating your board members and enlisting their help as champions will build your gift planning program by engaging them along with others in the mission of your organization.

◆ Like any piece of your strategy, activities that are led by your board and supported by you will go far when you take the time to educate and then motivate your board partners toward common goals to support the mission.

Chapter Seven

The Role of Volunteers

In This Chapter

···→ The role of volunteers

···→ Engaging volunteers to share your mission

···→ Invest in your volunteer program

···→ How do you measure success?

Like board members, other volunteers need to be educated about gift planning and why it can be an effective part of your organization's development program. Again, if they can consider personal gifts, their commitment will be greater and their impact will lead to greater success from their efforts.

Most gift planning programs do very little to engage loyal volunteers outside of board members. To build an effective program, consider the following:

◆ What groups make up your loyal volunteer base?

◆ How can you create volunteer opportunities that engage these groups but are not unwieldy to manage?

◆ What return do you want from your investment in the volunteer groups?

◆ How will you measure success?

Engaging Volunteers to Share Your Mission

Once you determine who makes up your volunteer group, you may want to survey those individuals to determine volunteer opportunities that interest them. After all, it is better to let volunteers determine for themselves how they want to engage with your organization on an ongoing basis.

One Champion Turned on the Spigot

When I headed up the gift planning program at Middlebury College, we built up a cadre of class gift planning volunteers. There was one volunteer who set up a special giving vehicle that used to be referred to as a "spigot trust." Its name comes from the idea that the donor can turn the income on and off like a spigot when needed. (It is technically a net income charitable remainder unitrust with makeup provision.) The IRS later determined that donors had too much control and charities stopped using this tool. But during this time period, it was an accepted vehicle. This volunteer was so taken with the tool that he told everyone in his class, and everyone else he knew in other classes, about it. By the time he was done, we had nearly twenty spigot trusts on the books, each with over $100,000 in it proving once again that just one champion can make a huge difference.

—Brian

 stories from the real world

Our generational research in *The Philanthropic Planning Companion* revealed that Traditionalists (born pre-1946) are happy to volunteer where you need them, including serving on committees, staffing the gift shop, or filling in where you asked. The Leading and Trailing Baby Boomers (born 1946–1964) want to be able to pick the areas where they provide volunteer support to a nonprofit. They are not willing to simply serve on the "golf committee" because that is where you need them. Because they started their families later in life than the generations before them, they generally have had less time to volunteer, and only in recent years have started to pick up the mantle from the Traditionalists. Generation X (born 1965–1976), typically wants to volunteer to work on the program they are supporting with their financial gifts. They have far less interest in volunteering for other institutional priorities. Millennials (born 1977–1984) tend not to volunteer for nonprofits unless they have a say in how the program they are volunteering for will be run. Millennials bring great energy and fresh, new ideas, but they also have the lowest tolerance for the bureaucracies found at most established nonprofits.

Invest in Your Volunteer Program

Once you establish your volunteer program and have identified the opportunities offered to volunteers, be sure to invest in it. Continue to provide staff and budget resources to make the program robust. Just as with gift planning stewardship programs, if you start and stop these efforts, you will lose your best volunteers and they may not continue as donors.

Make sure that you set clear measures of success for the program and report on them to the leadership of your nonprofit. The volunteer program must have a clear purpose and goals, and progress toward goals will ensure ongoing investment in the effort.

Volunteers are as American as apple pie and baseball and, when coupled with the generous nature of giving, can be a powerful force for change and growth in your organization.

To Recap

◆ Volunteers need to be educated about gift planning and why it can be an effective part of your organization's development program.

◆ Traditionalist volunteers (born pre-1946) are more likely to volunteer in areas where you need them, while New Philanthropists (born 1946 to present) want to volunteer in areas of interest to them.

◆ A successful volunteer program will bring your best donors closer to your organization and cultivate wonderful relationships with future donors.

◆ A weak volunteer program will alienate your best donors and make it less likely that prospects will invest in your mission.

> No matter how big and powerful government gets and the many services it provides, it can never take the place of volunteers.
>
> —President Ronald Reagan, 40th president of the United States

Chapter Eight

The Role of Professional Advisors

In This Chapter

- ···→ Types and roles of professional advisors in the planning process
- ···→ What you need to know to work with professional advisors
- ···→ Knowing when to call in a professional advisor
- ···→ Building relationships with professional advisors

It used to be that experienced gift planners were an excellent source of asset management opportunities for financial services professionals. In fact, the financial services industry relied upon charitable gift planners for information about gift planning tools and techniques. Charitable organizations were the gift planning experts from the 1950s through the 1990s. Gift planning advisory boards were wonderful outlets to share the technical know-how and provided user-friendly ways for professional advisors to enhance their clients' tax-planning strategies. Both groups enjoyed a mutually beneficial relationship.

After the enactment of the Tax Reform Act of 1986, all of that began to change. Under the act, the vast majority of tax shelters were removed from the code, leaving tax-planning professionals scrambling to find alternative ways to help their clients avoid taxes. The largest tax avoidance mechanism became the charitable deduction, which led to significant growth in personnel in the financial services sector with expertise about charitable giving.

With the growth of the financial services industry, professional advisors often now have the same information that was previously provided by gift planners. Many even list "charitable gift planning" on their lists of services. However, services such as charitable remainder trusts and private family foundations are offered more for the tax advantages than for the outcomes that could come from an "investment" in social capital. So for today's gift planner considering a gift planning advisory board, enlisting the interest of professional advisors can be more challenging.

According to several research studies, the number of donors who reported learning about the most basic planned gift option—a charitable bequest—from their legal or financial advisors has increased dramatically from the 1990s to today. Nearly three-quarters of charitable remainder trust donors report learning about the option from their advisors. An increasing number of planned gifts are being structured by professional advisors, and very often, charity is not included in their conversations.

By forming a working relationship with financial advisors, you educate an important influence in the eyes of donors. Familiarity with nonprofit services, donor motivations for giving, and charitable gift options and tools can expand the knowledge of the professional advisor. Advisors and gift planners can be successful when they can structure the right gift, with the right asset, at the right time, toward the right project, for the right cause.

Types and Roles of Professional Advisors in the Planning Process

Attorney: An attorney often specializes in a specific area of law. Most had only one course during law school where they learned about bequests—Wills 101. Trust and estate attorneys (aka. T&E attorneys), however, have dedicated their practice to learning and maintaining knowledge in this area. T&E attorneys prepare wills, trusts, and other documents that can create the opportunity for a significant gift. Elder law attorneys can also be helpful with end-of-life issues for your aging donors.

Accountant: Whether public accountants or certified public accountants (CPAs), this group generally knows about the tax law as it relates to charitable deductions and the tax advantages of being philanthropic. Accountants are helpful in explaining to prospects the tax implications of their gifts. You will find that for many prospects, their CPAs are their most trusted advisors for charitable giving questions.

Financial planner: Whether a financial planner or Certified Financial Planner (CFPs), these individuals can coordinate overall planning for a client/donor.

Consultant: Chartered Financial Consultants (ChFCs) are usually insurance professionals who can offer advice about financial options. ChFCs can also be found in banking and financial services.

Real estate professional: Realtors can be helpful in valuation of appreciated real estate and in the sale of gifted properties.

Insurance agent: Chartered Life Underwriters (CLUs) are the most knowledgeable of the insurance professionals. When it is important to replace the assets that are providing a significant gift to charity while also minimizing estate taxes, a wealth replacement trust that is funded by life insurance will allow a family to both make a bigger gift to charity and also retain more of the asset for the next generation.

One of the best things that advisors and fundraisers can do is to educate their clients/donors so that they can come to understand their best opportunities for planning and giving.

> *People are generally better persuaded by the reasons which they have themselves discovered than by those which have come into their minds by others.*
>
> —Blaise Pascal, seventeenth century French philosopher

What Do You Need to Know to Work with Professional Advisors?

Education can go a long way toward building a bridge between you and professional advisors. Even though advisors have increased their knowledge of charitable gift planning, there are still many who do not specialize in this area and rarely deal with charitable gifts. Limited knowledge of charitable giving options can cause advisors to feel awkward about the subject, which may make them reticent to bring up charitable giving as an option. Without formal training and education in gift planning, many brilliant professionals are left unprepared to help their clients fulfill their wishes. The necessity of additional tax knowledge can also add to their anxiety. In the end, a lack of understanding about a concept can often lead to rejection. So taking the time to share concepts with those whom you engage can eliminate the challenge and build an important relationship as well.

There is a common misconception that charities and financial advisors have different motivations. Professional advisors often see you as someone desiring to separate clients from their resources while seeing themselves in the role of promoting asset preservation and conservation of personal resources. When you ask a donor for a gift, it appears to go against this asset-preservation responsibility. In addition, a professional advisor, particularly one who gets paid based on a percentage of assets under management, may perceive any gift to your organization as taking away from the bottom line for the advisor and the client.

There are two problems with this notion. First, the advisor may not have all of the donor's assets under management. In fact, it is highly unlikely. When instead of trying to protect an interest the advisor allows the donor to do what feels right and helps integrate philanthropy into tax, estate, and financial planning, that advisor becomes more trusted than other advisors. It makes it more likely that the donor will bring additional assets to this trusted advisor who put the donor's interests first.

Second, it assumes that we live in a world of scarcity, that there is a limited pie of resources, and if a slice goes to your cause, there will be less for the advisor and the donor. Those of us who have worked in the charitable sector know that this is not true. The world is, in fact, a place of abundance. The more that donors give away, the more that comes back to them. Sometimes it is financial wealth, but it also may come back in the form of social, human, or intellectual capital. Anyone who has experienced the joy of being a true philanthropist will share that giving money away can be one of the greatest experiences of our journey in life.

> ### Make Sure That the Advisor Is a Winner, Too
>
> Pay attention to how advisors are compensated. If a charitable gift will cause the advisor to lose money, it may not be endorsed. If there are ways to look out for the advisor and the donor, consider them. For example, if the gift is large enough, a charitable remainder annuity trust may serve the charity and donor just as well as a gift annuity, but the financial advisor can keep the assets under management. Consider the advisors as parties to the negotiation of the gift, with their own interests in the conversation.
>
>

When handled poorly, these opposing notions can put donors in the middle. Donors must clearly articulate their wishes so advisors can calculate the "value" of their charitable intent.

Be aware of the challenge that can appear when a gift is being developed and planned. Depending on how the donor was "discovered," the advisors can be leery of supporting a planned gift since the idea didn't originate with them. You need to encourage donors to urge collaboration among their advisors, including financial planners, accountants, attorneys, and insurance specialists, as well as the gift planner, in their charitable planning.

Although communication among advisors is often poor, each can positively support donative intent. When forces are combined, the result can bring about a wonderful combination of professionals.

With the donor's financial well-being and personal motivations to give as the common denominator, professionals from the for-profit and nonprofit worlds can work together toward a common goal.

When working with advisors, look for those who are charitably minded. There are several excellent programs for advisors to become certified in charitable planning or to express their desire to partner in charitable giving, including the Heritage Institute programs in Portland, Oregon (*theheritageinstitute.com*); the Chartered Advisor in Philanthropy (CAP) program offered by the American College in Philadelphia, Pennsylvania (*http://theamericancollege.edu/financial-planning/cap-philanthropy*); and Advisors in Philanthropy (AiP) in Chicago, Illinois (*advisorsinphilanthropy.org*).

Knowing When to Call In a Professional Advisor

If the idea of consulting with a donor's professional advisor doesn't enter into your conversations during the cultivation process naturally, then it can be wise to suggest it. The larger the gift, the more likely it will be that the skill of one or more advisors could be advantageous.

As a fundraiser, it is easy to become jaded when working with professional advisors. But we find that when we work with charitably minded people, they tend to gravitate toward charitably minded advisors. We have never worked on a substantial charitable gift that did not closely involve the professional advisors of the donor. In fact, when the advisors were not involved, the gift often didn't work out or was scuttled by the advisor at the last minute because it did not account for the donor's entire situation. If you embrace the partnership with advisors, it will result in wonderful things for your cause and your donor.

Build Meaningful Relationships with Professional Advisors

Just as with donors, success in working with professional advisors comes when you build a relationship based on trust and mutual respect. I met Rick as he lay in a hospital bed several years ago. I had been asked to visit him by a generous donor, and as I regularly do, I stopped by to say hello, offer encouragement, and ask if there was anything that I might do to make Rick's stay more pleasant. I had met Rick once prior, but his appreciation for the time that I took to stop by was evident in his face as we talked. I offered my cell phone number on my card and left it for him as I departed. Weeks later, Rick called to thank me for visiting and asked me to lunch so I could hear about what he does. We got together, and from our conversation, I heard about his personal philosophy and approach for his clients. He was a planner with integrity who seeks to achieve the best outcomes for his client in a holistic way. He recognized the value of charity for his clients and brings it up in his planning model. When I shared that I had a similar model that sought to encourage our donors to incorporate financial, tax, and estate planning into their charitable gift planning, it was clear that our approaches would complement each other. Since that initial meeting, I have attended several events to support Rick's practice and he has gotten involved with two committees that are meaningful for him due to his health care experience. I have been impressed with his demeanor when I have introduced him to our constituents and I have appreciated his referrals, as well. The relationship is still growing, and we feel like the other has done more to assist in each other's work.

—Robert

!
important

Building Relationships with Professional Advisors

If you work in a community or region where it is practicable, you should make an effort to build relationships with local professional advisors. It is far easier to establish trust around a gift conversation when the first time you are meeting the advisor is not in the midst of a gift discussion. The best tools for building these relationships are a philanthropic planning council and a professional advisors network.

A philanthropic planning council or gift planning advisory board is a group of up to two dozen professional advisors who are most committed and most intense about your organization's mission. Beyond that "closely held" group, there are many advisors who may show some interest and might interact with your organization from time to time. Creating a professional advisors network would allow them to network with both your organization and their fellow professionals.

The role of the philanthropic planning council is to provide you with help and advice as you build your gift planning program. These are the professional advisors closest to your cause. They can write and edit materials, suggest ways to engage the professional advisors network, and give you credibility with the professional advisor community. You help them by offering support to their practice and ensuring when their clients come to your charity to discuss gifts that the advisors will be brought to the table.

The role of the professional advisors network is information sharing. You, with the help of the council, provide the network with information about your charitable giving as an integrated part of tax, estate, and financial planning. At the same time, you share information about your cause and encourage the network

> ### Funeral Directors Provide Leads
>
> We have found that the most overlooked member of a philanthropic planning council is the funeral director. In this day and age, with preplanning of funerals, nonprofits get more leads on potential planned gifts from funeral directors than anyone else on the council or in the network.
>
> **observation**

Always Suggest Meeting with the Prospect's Advisors

Whenever I suggest an integrated planned giving solution to a prospect, I strongly encourage the prospect to share it with the prospect's advisor and even to have us all meet together. In most cases the prospect welcomes the joint conversation.

I recently worked on a gift of real estate from a significant benefactor who was very dedicated to the cause of this particular nonprofit. He wanted to donate his house, but continue to live there for a period of time (retained life estate). Once he had agreed to the idea in principle, he asked me what steps we should take next. I suggested that we meet with his attorney and tax advisor to discuss the legal and tax considerations of the gift. He looked at me and asked "You would do that?" Even this sophisticated philanthropist didn't expect me, as the representative of the charity, to work collaboratively with his advisors to complete the gift. Once I made the offer, he readily agreed. Over three months, I worked with his advisors to secure a $3.5 million gift of real estate.

Don't assume that prospects, no matter how sophisticated, will think to introduce you to their advisors. The best course of action is to suggest it.

—Brian

 **stories from the real world**

to share information about your nonprofit to interested clients. For more information on building a council and network, see Chapter Five of *The Philanthropic Planning Companion*.

To Recap

◆ Professional advisors are key members of the gift planning team.

◆ Knowledge of the skill sets of each group of professional advisors will give you a valuable resource.

◆ Understanding what motivates professional advisors and how they are paid will help you work with them successfully.

◆ The best tools for engaging advisors with your organization are the philanthropic planning council and the professional advisors network.

◆ Fostering relationships with professional advisors before there is a gift discussion fosters trust.

◆ The most significant gifts all involve a partnership among you, professional advisors, and the donor.

Part Three

Prospect Interaction

With the core infrastructure for your gift planning program in place, the next step is to identify your gift planning prospects, segment your list, and craft a plan for moving these prospects through your moves management process. This is the hands-on work of gift planning that requires you to proactively build relationships with identified prospects and to help them meet personal planning goals while supporting your nonprofit. Though it is often challenging, it is also the most rewarding part of gift planning work, as you get to work with people loyal to your cause who want to make a meaningful difference. Our best days are the days we get to help prospects turn their philanthropic dreams into reality while also securing the future for their families. We know that you will enjoy this experience as you build your gift planning program.

Chapter Nine

Identifying Gift Planning Prospects

In This Chapter

- ···→ Generational differences

- ···→ Understanding the demographics of your prospects

- ···→ Identifying and ranking a list of prospects

- ···→ Segmenting your list

Since all of our worldly possessions remain behind at death, almost everyone has a choice of creating a plan for disposition of their assets. Giving back to one's community and supporting charitable organizations is often an important consideration in the construction of an estate plan. For many, a planned gift is the most significant gift they will ever make, because it either helps them meet a personal planning objective, such as increased retirement income, or costs nothing until their death, when they can afford to part with the assets.

While almost everyone is a candidate for gift planning and, therefore, it is important to promote gift planning widely, certain individuals may be more open to the gift planning message than others. Several studies in the last decade have shown us that over 90 percent of planned gifts are made by donors who have given loyally to the annual fund or been consistent members in the organization. We refer to this group as the loyals. The very best of these are donors who have made fifteen or more gifts and have given in ten or more consecutive years.

Interestingly, less than 10 percent of identified loyal donors are rated as major gift prospects (ability to make a $100,000 gift over five years, or $20,000 per year) when you do a typical wealth screening. They are people who are off your radar and have not been actively cultivated or solicited for significant commitments to your nonprofit.

Gift planning prospects also do not view themselves as wealthy or as "philanthropists." Because the vast majority cannot make significant lifetime gifts, they do not seek the limelight and are not eager to share their intentions with you, which they see as modest. Yet this group of prospects names

> ### A Planned Gift Is Considerably Larger than an Annual Gift
>
> A planned gift is often the largest gift a person can make, sometimes one hundred times the value of an annual gift.
>
>

nonprofits as will beneficiaries with an average bequest size of approximately $50,000 nationally. For most nonprofits, that is indeed a major gift.

Generational Differences

In *The Philanthropic Planning Companion*, we identified significant generational differences when approaching philanthropy. For the last forty years, nonprofits built their fundraising operations, solicitation methods, and stewardship programs to appeal to the needs of the Depression, World War II, and Post-World generations, all born prior to 1946. We collectively called these generations the Traditionalists.

During that time, these cohorts were in their peak earning years. They had come of age at a time that gave them a profound sense of community and the need to be charitable. In 2010, the last of the Traditionalists reached the retirement age of sixty-five. While they will continue to be an important planned giving audience going forward, their influence and ability to give is now starting to wane.

To fill this void, the charitable community has already started to rely upon the Leading Boomers and the generations that follow to pick up the charitable mantle. We identified these generations together as the New Philanthropists. If you are to work effectively with these next generations of donors, you need a basic understanding of how they will react to fundraising and gift planning approaches. The same tools and ideas that worked for Traditionalists will not meet the needs of the New Philanthropists. And there are nuances for each generation within the two groups.

Defining Generations

Generational cohorts are defined by individuals who come of age (turning age seventeen to twenty-three) while experiencing the same set of cultural events. This causes them to develop a set of shared values that ties them together for the balance of their lives. Often they hold most dear things that were missing when they came of age. For example, those who came of age during the Great Depression value financial security.

> ### Take into Account How the Donor Wishes to Be Treated
>
> If your gift planning prospects do not see themselves as wealthy philanthropists, you need to account for this in your personal approaches and marketing to them. Otherwise, they will think that gift planning is "not for me." Remember, a donor-focused approach takes into account how the donor wishes to be treated.
>
> **observation**

Generation Name	Birth Years
Depression	1912–1921
World War II	1922–1927
Postwar	1928–1945
Leading Boomers	1946–1954
Trailing Boomers	1955–1964
Generation X	1965–1976
Millennials	1977–1984
Great Recession/Boomerang	1985–?

Social scientists have identified seven living generations in the United States, each with a unique set of shaping moments and shared values. An eighth generation, sometimes called the Boomerang generation, is just emerging.

To help understand each generational cohort, we created a table showing the shaping moments and values, along with the best gift planning approaches and marketing tips for each. To review a more detailed application of generational cohort theory to giving, please see *The Philanthropic Planning Companion.*

Depression (Born 1912–1921)	
Defining moment: ◆ Great Depression	Shared values: ◆ Practicality ◆ Savings ◆ Safety/security ◆ Friends/family ◆ Trust for charities
Best approaches: ◆ Bequests ◆ Unrestricted endowment ◆ Help the needy when tough times arrive ◆ Secure our future	Marketing tips: ◆ Simple/presented in a straightforward manner ◆ Use visuals and other cues ◆ Printed/face to face ◆ No reverse type

World War II (Born 1922–1927)	
Defining moment: ◆ World War II	Shared values: ◆ Patriotic ◆ Respect for authority ◆ Romantic ◆ Self-reliant ◆ Trust for charities
Best approaches: ◆ Save the world ◆ Delayed gratification ◆ Remembered for sacrifices ◆ "Immortality" ◆ Naming using bequests	Marketing tips: ◆ Concierge-level treatment ◆ Rebates/coupons/discounts ◆ Matching gifts/challenges ◆ Use print ◆ Families trust these individuals

Postwar (Born 1928–1945)	
Defining moments: ◆ End of World War II ◆ Strong economy ◆ Move to the suburbs ◆ Cold War/Korean War ◆ McCarthyism ◆ Emergence of rock and roll ◆ Civil rights movement	**Shared values:** ◆ The American Dream ◆ Conformity ◆ Stability ◆ Family ◆ Self-fulfillment ◆ Trust for charities
Best approaches: ◆ Current gifts ◆ Beneficiary designations ◆ Gift annuities	**Marketing tips:** ◆ Volunteer opportunities (not necessarily tied to gift) ◆ Active images ◆ Outcomes-based

While each of the Traditionalist cohorts is unique and, as a result, behaves differently, gift planning for this group has been largely the same. In fact, it was around the behavior of these three cohorts that gift planning programs have been built over the last forty years. For all of their differences, each of the Traditionalist cohorts came of age at times when they could trust nonprofits. If nonprofits showed that they had a valuable mission, the Traditionalists would support it, often with modest current gifts and larger gifts at death. Most of the time, these gifts were unrestricted, with the donor trusting the nonprofit to put the gift to good use where the need was greatest.

This all changed with the emergence of the New Philanthropists, starting with the Leading Boomers. These generational cohorts came of age at a time when trust for the establishment, government and nonprofits had waned. They are no longer willing to make unrestricted gifts and trust charities to put those gifts to use where the need is greatest. And they certainly don't want to make planned gifts that trust the nonprofit to use the money wisely when the donor has passed on.

The best approaches and marketing tips for the New Philanthropist cohorts show an increased

Don't Miss the Opportunity for Unrestricted Gifts

Brian and I are strong advocates for using a donor-focused approach with your donors and we offer suggestions for what we have found are the best concepts for each generation. While the Leading Boomers and the successive generations are now interested in restricting their giving, and we want to emphasize the importance of customizing your approach to each New Philanthropist, don't miss the opportunity to reach out to Traditionalists to close unrestricted gifts that support your mission. Like we show in our chart, I have been able to recently work with about a dozen donors from the Postwar cohort that want to support our hospitals with their gift.

—Robert

practical tip

dependence on gift planning through structured gifts. As explained in **Part Four**, the earning potential of each cohort in the New Philanthropists is lower than the generation that preceded it. If these prospects are to make gifts, it will require you to integrate their philanthropy into their tax, estate, and financial planning in such a way as to help them meet their personal financial goals and their charitable goals. The world has fundamentally changed.

Leading Boomers (Born 1946–1954)	
Defining moments: ◆ Assassinations of JFK, RFK, and MLK Jr. ◆ Vietnam War ◆ First man on the moon	**Shared values:** ◆ Personal/social expression ◆ Individualism protected ◆ Youth/health/wellness ◆ Lack of trust for charities
Best approaches: ◆ Social justice meets personal planning ◆ Restricted gifts ◆ Advisor partnerships ◆ Beneficiary designations ◆ Complex asset gifts ◆ Structured gifts	**Marketing tips:** ◆ Impact, outcomes, and verifiability ◆ Large type/high contrast/no glossy paper ◆ Fun, individualism, and excitement

Trailing Boomers (Born 1955–1964)	
Defining moments: ◆ Fall of Vietnam ◆ Watergate ◆ Nixon resignation ◆ Energy crisis	**Shared values:** ◆ Lonely individualism ◆ Cynicism/distrust ◆ Health and wellness ◆ Family commitments ◆ Lack of trust for charities
Best approaches: ◆ Gift outcomes ◆ Full range of charitable giving tools ◆ Restricted gifts ◆ Advisor partnerships	**Marketing tips:** ◆ Impact, outcomes, verifiability, and accountability ◆ Conscious of distrust ◆ Robust stewardship

Generation X (Born 1965–1976)	
Defining moments:	**Shared values:**
◆ Large national debt/stock market crash of 1987	◆ Free agency/independence
◆ Challenger explosion	◆ Dependence on friends
◆ Fall of the Berlin Wall	◆ Cynical about future
◆ First Persian Gulf War	◆ Street-smart
◆ AIDS crisis	◆ Quality of life
	◆ Accept violence/sex
	◆ Lack of trust for charities
Best approaches:	**Marketing tips:**
◆ Custom gift solutions	◆ Impact, outcomes, verifiability, accountability, and volunteer ops
◆ Beneficiary designations	◆ Not attractive or rich—facts
◆ Restricted gifts (almost exclusively)	◆ Subtlety/irony/irreverence
◆ Advisor partnerships	

Millennials (Born 1977–1984)	
Defining moments:	**Shared values:**
◆ The Internet	◆ Hopeful about financial future
◆ Good economic times	◆ Heightened fears
◆ Columbine High School shootings	◆ Change is good
◆ September 11 terrorist attacks	◆ Tolerance/diversity
◆ Wars in Iraq and Afghanistan	◆ Lack of trust for charities
Best approaches:	**Marketing tips:**
◆ Beneficiary designations	◆ "Get out of the way"
◆ Restricted gifts exclusively	◆ Change it up
◆ Modest annual donations focused on mission	◆ Fresh and multichannel
	◆ Brand-conscious/loyal

Women and Men

Traditionally gift planning, along with other forms of philanthropy, was focused on men. Men had been the primary breadwinners and controlled charitable giving. Upon their death, wives would support the causes dictated by the husbands. However, we are seeing a significant shift in behavior with the New Philanthropists. Many more women consider themselves philanthropists than ever before. They are embracing the role and making giving decisions on their own, which may be different from their husbands' giving decisions. New Philanthropist women are also directing their gifts differently than New Philanthropist men. Women are focused on giving money based on their values and desire to transform society, while men continue to focus more on capital projects.

Both men and women in the New Philanthropists are looking for more immediate outcomes. Women, however, are more concerned than men about outliving their resources, even when those resources are substantial. In many cases, a planned gift may be more attractive to a woman than a man because she can use it to help secure her financial future as well as support her favorite cause, even if it defers support for that cause.

> ### Men and Women Approach Charitable Giving Differently. Who Knew?
>
> There is an entire field of research on the differences between men and women in their charitable giving, including an overlay on the generational cohorts. To learn more, visit *http://bit.ly/womens-philanthropy.*
>
>

Age and Wealth

For years, it was assumed that old, wealthy people made planned gifts. Following that rule of thumb, nonprofits actively encouraged old, wealthy people to consider planned gifts and most planned gifts came from that group. However, as more studies of giving preference and behavior have been completed, we have discovered that old, wealthy people make planned gifts not because they are old and wealthy, but because they are loyal. In fact, once someone reaches age sixty, the likelihood of that person even considering a new charity for a planned gift is less than 10 percent. However, if the donor is already engaged by a nonprofit by the age of sixty or has a life-changing event (such as a cancer diagnosis), then, of course, the donor is a strong planned giving prospect.

Correlation Model vs. Loyalty Model. Which One Is More Predictive?

Several years ago, I was approached by a vendor who was developing a predictive model for planned giving and needed data on our planned giving prospects. Several months later, he came back with his model. It was very complicated and used outside resources to add wealth, other charities supported, age, and a multitude of other factors. He shared with no small amount of pride that his new model was predictive to 70 percent of known planned giving donors. That is, when he ran his model against our database, it ranked 70 percent of our known planned gift donors as gift planning prospects.

We then showed him our loyalty model, which was over 90 percent predictive. He explained that our model might work for our database, but that by adding all these other factors, his model should be more effective. We then tried our model with other nonprofits and it maintained its 90 percent predictive standard.

It turns out that his model put a significant weight on age, since most planned giving donors in the databases he analyzed were older. So a prospect with no giving history and age ninety would get a higher score than a sixty-year-old with twenty years of giving history. Just because something correlates (many charities have legacy societies filled with older prospects) doesn't mean that it is predictive.

—Brian

Similarly, wealthy people also do not make as many planned gifts unless they are also loyal. Wealth is not predictive of gift planning. When you consider that over 90 percent of planned gift donors are not wealthy, it becomes apparent that we should not use wealth to identify our gift planning audience.

Donors without Heirs

The 2008 study by Adrian Sargeant and Jen Shang, *Identification, Death, and Bequest Giving,* found that among the loyal donors, those most likely to make future gifts are individuals without any children. These are individuals who want their lives to have meaning and have no natural heirs. By supporting nonprofits, they accomplish this goal.

Identifying and Ranking a List of Prospects

You can spend thousands of dollars for a vendor to evaluate your database for gift planning prospects. However, finding them is as easy as pulling a list of your loyal donors and ranking them by the length of time they have supported your organization. To create your initial list of prospects most open to a gift planning message, review your database to find donors who have given according to this matrix.

Rating	Description
1	Known planned gift donors
2	Prospects who have inquired about gift planning in the past but are not captured in rating 1
3	Donors who have given fifteen or more times but are not captured in ratings 1 and 2
4	Donors who have given ten of the last fifteen years but are not captured in ratings 1 through 3
5	Donors who have given seven of the last ten years but are not captured in ratings 1 through 4
6	Donors who have given five of the last seven years but are not captured in ratings 1 through 5
7	Donors who have given three of the last five years but are not captured in ratings 1 through 6
8	Current or former board members not captured in ratings 1 through 7
9	Long-term volunteers and those tied to the organization long term through personal or family associations not captured in ratings 1 through 8
10	Current or former staff members with at least some giving history who are not captured in ratings 1 through 9
11	Donors and prospects previously rated 1 through 10 who fall off the rating system when ratings are reviewed (typically every other year)
12	Donors who have turned down gift planning asks but really are saying "not now" (qualified prospects)
13	Prospects who have been identified and qualified, but it is clear they will never make a future gift (i.e., do not solicit for planned gifts)

While this ranking is a starting point, you should adjust it, particularly rankings 8 through 10, for your nonprofit. For example, if you are a membership organization such as a museum, many of your members might see membership as a gift. In the typical museum, there are tiers of membership. Members who are loyal are those who maintain their memberships over time at a level above what would make economic sense from the benefits of membership.

Your ranked list is a propensity or inclination rating for gift planning. Once you establish it, you should add the ratings to your database. This gives you a baseline group of loyals from which to develop your segmented visit and marketing lists.

Segmenting Your List

Segmenting your loyals for gift planning purposes is more of an art than a science. We have worked with nonprofits that create an actual matrix for this purpose, but you'll need to decide how you want to use the different segmentation options to guide your efforts. How you do this will depend in no small part on the type of gifts you hope your prospects will consider and the makeup of your prospect pool.

Segmentation tools for gift planning include generational cohorts (age), gender, wealth, and no children. If your nonprofit needs planned gifts to mature quickly, you might segment by generational cohort and approach the Traditionalists first.

If you want to limit the number of times you are turned down for a gift, you might elect to approach more women or more individuals without children, who (among the loyals) tend to be more open to the gift planning message.

If you want to maximize the dollars from each gift you complete, you might approach those with the greatest gift capacity or wealth indicators.

Of course, you can also put these together so that you approach the most loyal, wealthy women with no children from the Traditionalists first, which would likely give you the fastest results in the largest amounts. By focusing on your donors and your nonprofit, you'll be able to identify the best method for you.

Once you establish your organization's priorities from its gift planning program, it is a relatively easy task to segment the list using these tools and begin to build relationships with these identified prospects one on one.

To Recap

◆ Gift planning prospects are drawn from
your regular, consistent donors known as "loyals."

◆ Gift planning prospects typically do not show up in wealth screenings and do not see
themselves as wealthy.

◆ Always identify and rank your loyal prospects before segmenting your list.

◆ Segment gift planning prospects by generational cohorts, gender, wealth, and lack of heirs.

◆ Select which segments to approach first based upon your organization's priorities.

Chapter Ten

Approaching Your Prospects

In This Chapter

---→ Creating prospect strategies using a donor-focused approach

---→ Qualifying identified gift planning prospects

---→ Types of visits

---→ Using gift planning tools to meet personal planning objectives

With your segmented prospect list in hand, you are ready to start putting together prospect strategies for your top prospects and plugging them into your moves management process. While this may seem daunting at first, remember that these are not cold calls on people who have no interest in your nonprofit. These are wonderful philanthropists (even if they do not see themselves that way) who have made regular, consistent investments in the cause for years. Their single biggest objection to a visit will be, "Why do you want to see me? Don't you want to see people who can make big gifts?" To which you can answer, "I just want to come by and say thank you for being a longtime supporter and hear more about why you are so passionate about what we do."

Do not overload your portfolio with gift planning prospects right off the bat. As discussed in **Part Two**, you can handle only a certain number of prospects, visits, and activity. If you are already a full-time fundraiser, you'll need to replace some of your existing prospects with gift planning prospects or integrate gift planning work into your conversations with your existing prospects. If you are not a full-time fundraiser, you have to give something else up to pursue this work. It is important to give it the time and attention it deserves. Keep in mind that even if you are successful starting gift planning conversations, it often takes several visits, frequently over a period of years, to convert these conversations into commitments—and those commitments into matured gifts at the death of the donor. Be sure to measure your success by activity and not by dollars raised, especially in the early years.

Creating Prospect Strategies Using a Donor-focused Approach

Most fundraisers are never trained to put together a prospect strategy or educated about moves management. This makes fundraising and gift planning much more difficult.

Creating Prospect Strategies

A prospect strategy is your plan for approaching an identified prospect and developing a relationship over time. It does not have to be more than a paragraph or two in length, but it keeps you on track as you build trust with your prospect. The strategy normally includes:

◆ The prospect's connection to your nonprofit

◆ Why you have identified the person as a prospect at this time

◆ Areas of interest at your nonprofit

◆ Who has the best connections with the prospect and should be on the prospect development team

◆ Who is best suited to introduce you to the prospect, if needed

◆ How you hope to engage the prospect to build the relationship (invite to events, introduce to key people, share reports, give private tours, etc.)

◆ Potential issues that may stand in the way of building a relationship and how you plan to overcome them

◆ Known personal planning objectives that might be integrated into the strategy

◆ Names of professional advisors (if known) who counsel the prospect

◆ Current stage in your moves management process

◆ Timeline for progressing through moves management to ask for an investment in the cause

As you take on gift planning prospects, put together a prospect strategy for each one and record it in your database. It will keep you on track and will inform others in your organization (and those who come after you) of your plan for the prospect.

Developing Your Moves Management Approach

A prospect strategy is just the beginning. Next you need to plug your gift planning prospects into your moves management process. If your nonprofit does not have one, we strongly encourage you to adopt one. There are great resources on this topic at *instituteforgiving.org* or in Chapter Seven of *The Philanthropic Planning Companion.*

A basic moves management approach includes these steps:

Identification/education: Process of identifying suspects (potential prospects) through peer review, referrals, research, database screening, marketing responses, and attendance at events, and then sharing information about the mission of the nonprofit to engage them in your work.

Qualification: Process of evaluating an identified suspect to determine if the suspect has both the capacity and inclination to become a prospect. If not, will the suspect have such capacity in the future, or can a relationship with

If a Tree Falls in the Forest...

If you do not record activity in the database, it is as though it never happened.

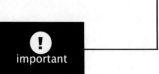
important

the suspect be developed to increase propensity for the future?

Cultivation: Process of building a relationship between prospects and your nonprofit to engage them and to learn about their passions.

Solicitation: Process of approaching prospects to ask them to consider increasing their level of involvement with your nonprofit through a significant gift commitment to support an area they are passionate about while also meeting personal planning objectives for themselves and their families.

Most Prospects Will Start in the Cultivation Phase

Because you have already identified and qualified your gift planning prospects, most of your prospects will start in the cultivation phase of your moves management process.

Negotiation: Ongoing process of solicitation, after the "ask" has been made, to find the right fit among the prospect's passions, personal planning objectives, and your nonprofit's objectives. This process includes the creation of a carefully crafted gift agreement, with the responsibilities of both parties clearly defined, using the help of professional advisors.

Stewardship: A donor-focused process where your nonprofit provides a contemporaneous thank-you within seven days, indicates in the thank-you what the gift was used for, reports back to the donor within six months on the long-term outcome the gift has created or will create, recognizes the gift publicly (when desired), and provides ongoing support and connection as cultivation toward additional gifts. Stewardship is covered in more detail in **Chapter Twelve**.

If you do have a moves management process in place, plug your gift planning prospects into the right moves management step and begin to move them along as you would other prospects in your system. The exact system used is less important than actually having a system and using it.

Qualifying Identified Gift Planning Prospects

With your pool of prospects identified and strategies in place, you can now begin to visit with the identified prospects and qualify them one-on-one. Through the qualifying process, you help the prospect identify passions and personal planning needs that may stand in the way of making a more substantial investment in the cause. It also allows you to build a relationship between the prospect and the nonprofit. For most prospects, this starts with the personal qualifying visit.

Qualifying Visits

Probably the most difficult prospect visit to schedule and handle is the qualifying visit. Until an identified suspect has been qualified, the organization cannot pursue a meaningful relationship. While many fundraisers hope that research can fill this role, the reality is that a fundraiser can learn more in a single qualification visit than a researcher can discover in hours of work.

Fundraising, Not "Friendraising"

When building a relationship with a prospect, always remember that it is a relationship between the prospect and the nonprofit, not a personal relationship between you and the prospect. While a personal relationship may also develop, you should focus on connecting the prospect to passions related to your cause and to other people working for your nonprofit so that there are multiple points of contact. This way, should you leave your position, the relationship with the organization remains.

Obtaining Qualifying Visits

Obtaining a qualifying visit is not as simple as picking up the telephone. While that might have worked back when only a few nonprofits were visiting prospects, those days have long passed. Today, you must be strategic when seeking to obtain qualifying visits. We recommend a four-step approach:

1. *Prepare the prospect for the call.* Most people today won't pick up the phone if they do not recognize who is calling. Start by sending a personal note or email on the nonprofit's letterhead introducing yourself and explaining that you will be calling to arrange a visit.

> ### Qualifying Visits Can Be Fun!
>
> Qualifying visits can be fun if you enjoy getting to know people. As a fundraiser, it should be one of your favorite things to do.
>
> **observation**

2. *Prepare to make the call.* Before picking up the phone, review your written file and database, including your strategy for this prospect. If you have peers who might share information, ask them. You want to know why you are calling and their connection to the nonprofit.

3. *Place the call.* Stand and smile when you make the call. It projects energy and enthusiasm. These actions are clearly perceived by the person taking your call.

4. *Handle the objections.* There are several common objections when calling loyals to ask for a first visit. You should be prepared to answer these objections as well as any others that may be unique to your charity's situation.

Indifference to the Mission

If a donor is going to move from being a loyal supporter to a true investor in the cause through a planned gift, the individual needs to have a passion for some aspect of the mission. If the donor is not passionate about some aspect of the mission and is motivated to make the occasional gift because a friend has requested it, it will be difficult to get that individual to take a meeting. There is tremendous value in having this conversation regardless of whether the donor takes the meeting or not. If by having the conversation you learn that the donor is not a gift planning prospect, you can move the prospect off your list as a "13." (See the table on page 64.)

Rebuilding Bridges

I took a new job working directly for a nonprofit. My first month, I was making a series of calls to schedule qualifying visits. I was turned down over and over again. I finally asked someone why they wouldn't take the visit, and the person unloaded a rant to end all rants about the dissolution of the fraternity system. I made it a habit to ask why whenever I was rejected for a visit and quickly learned the hot-button items for that nonprofit. I then found out why it had done what it did, so I could explain the situation to these prospects. Thereafter, I had a much easier time getting my qualifying visits.

—Brian

stories from the real world

Lack of Effectiveness

There are large numbers of donors who have a passion for an aspect of your mission but make only modest gifts because they believe you are not doing a good job meeting it. There are countless reasons that donors may believe this about your nonprofit—from bad reports in the press to something a peer said, information provided by a competing nonprofit, etc. Until your donor shares this information, it will be impossible for you to move the conversation forward. Use the phone call to identify and acknowledge the issue. You can then discuss it more fully on the visit.

Culling the List

Qualifying prospects includes the step of moving a suspected prospect off your list. It frees you to add a new prospect to the list to be qualified.

important

Personal Circumstances

Most gift planning donors do not see themselves as having the ability to make major charitable gifts. The very term *major gifts* is off-putting to a large portion of this audience. A donor receiving a call from a major gift officer is likely to cite personal circumstances as the reason for being unable to meet. After all, the donor does not want to meet with a fundraiser and then have to share that he or she does not have the capacity to make a gift at that level. It is better not to meet at all.

When placing these calls, you should reinforce for donors that the visits are to thank them for their loyalty, share more about the charity's mission, and learn about why the donors are passionate about that mission. The gift conversation will come later, if a donor has the capacity and inclination. If the donor expresses concerns about personal circumstances that would stand in the way of making a gift, you need to share, if the conversation reaches that point, that you have tools available to help the donor meet personal planning objectives while also supporting the mission. The balance of the conversation can happen on the visit; just put the donor at ease so that the visit can happen.

Too Busy/Scheduling Conflicts

You often deal with donors who simply do not have the time to meet. It is up to you to find a time that the donor does not realize is available and use it to schedule the meeting and move the conversation forward. This usually occurs one of two ways—first, the donor has a life event, crisis, or unfortunate circumstance and decides to make planning a priority. These are the times when it is very important for you to have relationships with advisors. If the donor appears on the advisor's doorstep and asks to do planning because of the birth of a child, the death of a loved one, a change in employment, retirement, the graduation of the last child from college, the pending sale of a closely held/family business, or another life event, the donor is likely not thinking about your nonprofit. But if you have a good relationship with the donor's advisors, the advisor is much more likely to remind the donor to

---

Empathy

Throughout our careers, we have often encountered donors who have shared issues about the organization we have represented. In almost every case, by being empathetic and listening to the donor, we have not only been able to understand their perspective but have also then been able to suggest a way to improve upon the issue and overcome their objection. If you share the passion of your donors in the organization that you work for, you can see these challenges as opportunities.

observation

> ### Just Your Name and Organization Will Do
>
> We are all proud of the titles we earn in our roles with our organizations, but when we are making our calls, sharing our name and the name of our organization is usually enough to establish credibility with the donor.
>
>

include charitable intentions in planning and bring you into the conversation. For more on the life events that cause prospects to complete planned gifts, see Chapter Seven of the *Resource Book.*

The second way that these meetings happen is on the fly. Donors make time to attend charity events, serve on boards, eat meals, coach kids' sports, and a myriad of other activities. If you can find a way to piggyback on these commitments, it may be possible to get the conversation started. Once the discussion has momentum, a donor passionate about an aspect of your mission will take the subsequent phone calls and meetings required to complete the gift. The key is to make it as simple and easy as possible for the donor to begin the process.

Planning for Qualifying Visits

The qualifying visit allows you to learn more about the capacity, passions, and personal planning objectives of the donor. Be sure to have a written agenda for your qualifying meeting, including what you hope to accomplish and learn in the session.

Conducting Qualifying Visits

During qualifying visits, ask open-ended questions and listen carefully for what is being said as well as what is not being said. Chapter Seven of the *Resource Book* contains a list of sample qualifying-visit questions, which are designed to get donors talking. These questions are broken into three categories, including general questions, capacity questions, and propensity questions.

At the end of the qualifying visit, you should thank the donor, summarize the meeting, and articulate next steps. A qualifying visit should not end until there is a clearly defined next step with the prospect or the prospect has been disqualified and can be removed from the gift planning prospect list.

Following Up Qualifying Visits

Be sure to follow up your qualifying visit with a thank-you note within forty-eight hours. If you are on a multi-day trip, the thank-you note should be written and sent from the road. There will be an opportunity to send

> ### Three Strikes and They're Out!
>
> When you travel nationally, it is possible to use your travel schedule itself to disqualify prospects. Begin by determining who from your assigned prospect pool you need to visit this year. Put together a travel schedule for the entire year, allowing you to get to those cities multiple times to meet the number of prospects in each. When you call for a visit, if the prospect is not available, provide the next set of dates you'll be in town. Once a prospect has turned down three sets of dates, it is likely that the prospect simply does not want to visit with you. Disqualify the prospect and move on to others on your list. Since you'll be filling multiple trips to the same city in just one set of phone calls, this will allow you to make fewer calls and fill your entire travel schedule over the course of the year.
>
>

a more formal follow-up letter when you return to the office. For Gen Xers and Millennials, it may be more appropriate to use an email thank-you, depending upon the donor. Keep in mind, however, that even if a written thank-you seems trite to a Gen X or Millennial donor, it will make the visit more memorable.

Make it your policy to record information about the visit as quickly as possible after it happens. There are many voice recording applications available for smartphones that allow you to record what happened as soon as you leave a meeting. Some databases even have mobile apps that you can use to record your visit notes. Try to record these items after a qualifying visit:

◆ Background on the donor, including family members, family history, and personal and professional bios

◆ Sense of engagement and history with your nonprofit

◆ Areas of interest about which the donor is passionate

◆ Where the areas of interest falls on the donor's philanthropic priorities

◆ Other nonprofits the donor supports

◆ Capacity of the donor or observations of wealth from the visit (type of car, house, art, and other assets)

◆ Personal planning objectives the donor has that may impact philanthropic planning

◆ Names of any professional advisors mentioned

◆ Answers to questions written up prior to the visit

◆ What the donor agreed to do

◆ What you agreed to do

◆ Next steps and timeline for completion

Once this information has been compiled, you should complete the follow-up steps in a timely way and remind the donor of any action items. Following up the visit will rarely be the donor's first priority, so appropriate reminders will go a long way toward moving the process forward to cultivation.

Cultivation Visits

The cultivation visit should be a logical progression from the qualifying visit. Use the cultivation visit to further quantify the donor's particular areas of interest and passion for the mission, discover other charities the donor supports and why, ask about personal planning objectives the donor has that might stand in the way of philanthropy, and inquire how the donor uses professional advisors.

When in Rome...

I am constantly reminded that to work in a donor-focused way requires us to think of the things that will make donors comfortable. This thought should always be front of mind when you are visiting with your donors. Consider how you are dressed...can you take off your jacket if they are dressed casually? If they offer a beverage, do you join them and accept their hospitality? Do you ask open-ended questions and then actively listen as they share a proud story about their children or grandkids? Brian and I could share several fun stories about visits where we enjoyed the time spent with our donors. If we are to embrace being donor-focused, we need to follow the lead of our host on our visits.

—Robert

 practical tip

By the end of the visit, you should have clear action steps for moving the donor's relationship forward. It may be the introduction of additional staff people or volunteers, attendance at an event, or participation in an activity. The key is to use the cultivation visit to identify how the donor wants to be engaged and to provide that level of engagement, deepening the relationship over time.

It may take several cultivation visits to move a donor from the cultivation phase to the solicitation phase. It should not take years and years to reach the solicitation phase with most donors. If it does, you need to revisit your strategy and visit planning worksheet to ensure that each visit is moving the cultivation toward a planned gift.

I Give

One of the best things that I have done in my career was to make a gift to each organization that I have represented. Not only did it cause me to consider the mission that I spoke about daily, but it also gave me an understanding of the donor's perspective and giving experience. Brian and I both believe in this philosophy and Brian regularly makes accommodations for his clients through his donor-advised fund. I am proud to represent organizations I believe in and feel there is no more powerful phrase to use when asking than, "Would you consider joining me with your gift?"

—Robert

 stories from the real world

---

A Word about Philanthropic Planning

In our first book, *The Philanthropic Planning Companion,* we suggest that nonprofits adopt a philanthropic planning model, particularly for their top-rated, principal gift prospects. These are individuals with the greatest capacity and inclination toward your mission who can make institution-changing gifts, including planned gifts.

Ideally nonprofits and advisors would have the time, volunteers, and staff to work with all philanthropists equally. But with limited resources, nonprofits and advisors need to provide the highest level of attention to those philanthropists who are capable of making the most meaningful and institution-changing gifts, as charitable giving by high-net-worth households to nonprofit organizations accounts for about two-thirds of all individual giving and half of all charitable giving in the United States. These individuals are fully integrating their philanthropy into their overall tax, estate, and financial planning—crafting meaningful legacies to benefit both their families and the causes they love.

As you build your gift planning program, you will grow into these kinds of conversations. But as we noted early on, your first conversations will be far more basic. Focus on the mission of your nonprofit and the goals of your prospects. You'll find that simple planned gifts will make up 80 percent of the gift planning receipts you realize. Then you will add some of the more complex vehicles described in **Part One** of the *Resource Book,* such as the charitable gift annuity and charitable remainder trust. As the program gains sophistication, you'll eventually offer some of the truly complex planning tools, such as charitable lead trusts and wealth replacement trusts, that help families with the most significant means. While we would love for you to start with philanthropic planning, always begin with the most basic options. Most of the gifts will be found there anyway.

Using Gift Planning Tools to Meet Personal Planning Objectives

As you have cultivation discussions with donors from your segmented list, you will begin to hear the same thing over and over: "I would like to make a gift, but . . ." Gift planning provides you with a wealth of tools to overcome that objection. The key to success is not to try to sell your donors on tools but to talk to them about your mission. Then you can apply the tools to help them meet their personal planning goals while also being charitable. In **Part Four**, we discuss how you use these same approaches in marketing your gift planning program.

Crafting Your Legacy

When surveyed, most loyals want to create a meaningful legacy during their lifetime and then cap it off with an estate commitment to ensure they are remembered after they are gone. They want to make a lasting difference and some remembrance that they were here. Basic tools, such as naming your nonprofit as the beneficiary of a will, retirement plan, life insurance policy, donor-advised fund, payable-on-death account, or transfer-on-death asset, allow your prospect to set up that ultimate legacy gift without any cost today. And it is an easy conversation to have.

Increasing Your Retirement Income

The Traditionalists were savers and frequently have pensions. They should have enough resources to support their retirement, yet they worry that they may not have enough. One way to help them overcome this fear is to offer a gift plan that will provide them with similar or greater income as the assets they are donating. The charitable gift annuity, charitable remainder trusts, and pooled income funds can meet this need.

Interestingly, because the New Philanthropists will have fewer savings for retirement and only a few will benefit from pensions, they are also looking for ways to increase their future income in retirement. Tools such as the flexible/deferred gift annuity and the flip charitable remainder unitrust are good ways to meet this goal.

The Million-dollar Dog

This gift was definitely not a dog. I was recently working with an entrepreneurial philanthropist who wanted to make the first million-dollar gift from a living donor to a particular organization in support of our furry friends. She is planning to sell her business in about four years, and ultimately the vast majority of her estate will go to the same nonprofit. We discussed a gift of a share of the business followed by redemption of the stock by the corporation, but it did not fit with the succession plan for the business. She had the assets to make an outright gift and could use a deduction this year, but she raised the concern that if her business did not sell for as much as she anticipated, she might be short on income in retirement.

In collaboration with her advisors, I recommended a flexible payment gift annuity, with payments starting between four and twenty years from now. At the time of the sale of her business, she will be able to decide if she needs additional income. If she is 100 percent sure she does not need any additional income, she can relinquish her right to payments from the flexible gift annuity and take an additional income tax charitable deduction. If she is unsure, she can wait to start payments until she needs them. This gives her the flexibility to make her gift now while providing her with income security in retirement.

A few days after we reviewed these figures, a beautiful, female pit pull walked up to the door of the nonprofit wearing an "adopt me" jacket. Pinned to the jacket was a $1 million gift to fund the flexible gift annuity. A true million-dollar dog.

—Brian

stories from the real world

Paying for College for Your Children or Grandchildren

Many of your identified prospects will have children or grandchildren approaching college age. With college costs skyrocketing at a rate much higher than inflation, covering these costs can be a major financial challenge that keeps individuals from making gifts to support your cause. The best tool to save for college is still the 529 college savings plan. But if your prospect truly wants to be charitable, you can also offer commuted payment gift annuities or a term-of-years flip charitable remainder unitrust.

Providing Income to Your Elderly Parents

A growing number of families need to provide for their children and for their elderly parents, because the parents' retirement savings were hurt by economic conditions or they simply have outlived them. Frequently there are issues where the parent does not want to take money from the child, even though the parent needs the help. You can help your prospect solve this problem with a charitable gift annuity payable to the parent. Because the check comes from your nonprofit and not the prospect directly, the parent is much less likely to be upset and more likely to take the payment.

Maximizing Your Children's or Grandchildren's Inheritance

For most loyals, a charitable gift is third on the list of personal priorities, after making sure that their own needs are met and their family's future is secure. By acknowledging this in your conversation with the prospect, it relieves donors of the idea that you want to separate them from their money at the expense of their kids. You can offer them charitable lead annuity trusts or a wealth-replacement charitable remainder trusts, which allows them to make a significant charitable gift and secure the inheritance of their heirs.

Creating a Family Vision and Multigenerational Plan

Values-based planning has become a significant side industry in the financial planning world. The New Philanthropists have embraced the idea of multigenerational planning for wealth and social welfare of their families. It is one of the reasons we wrote *The Philanthropic Planning Companion*-to help fundraisers understand and embrace the need for this kind of thinking. But as we noted earlier, you probably won't get to this right away. If you have prospects that need this type of work, look for professional advisors who have the Chartered Advisor in Philanthropy (CAP) designation and consider referring them to *Inspired Philanthropy* by Tracy Gary. Gary's book has a series of questionnaires and tools to help the philanthropists develop their own philanthropic plans.

No matter the personal planning objective, if the prospect is truly charitable, there is a solution you can offer. When prospects turn down all the charitable options, it probably means that they just do not want to make gifts, and the personal planning issues are just ways to say no.

Are You Certified?

Although special certifications are not required to do gift planning work, many employers look for a law degree, CFP, Certified Specialist in Planned Giving (CSPG), Chartered Advisor in Philanthropy (CAP), or other indications that you are qualified as a gift planner. A good place to start may be the Certified Fundraising Executive (CFRE) program. It ensures that you develop a strong background in all aspects of fundraising, including gift planning, and then you can move on to some of the more sophisticated specialties. Both of us attained the CFRE designation, and it illustrates to the fundraising and professional advisor worlds that we take our profession seriously.

practical tip

Events that Prompt Gift Planning Opportunities

Gift planning opportunities often arise when individuals contemplate changing their overall tax, estate, and financial planning. Fundraising campaigns are designed to highlight opportunities to support your mission and create deadlines for prospects, thereby causing them to act even if there is no other external cause for them to consider their long-term plans. However, often the best time for an individual to consider a planned gift is as a result or in contemplation of a significant event or life transition. In Chapter Seven of the *Resource Book*, we provide you with a list of life events that trigger gift planning. Listen for these as you complete your cultivation visits. If an opportunity presents itself, you may have to accelerate your schedule and move to a solicitation sooner than originally planned.

Integration with Other Areas of Development

As mentioned in **Part Two**, gift planning does not happen in a vacuum. You work collaboratively with other areas in the fundraising shop to achieve donor goals. If you are doing your job well, you will be involved in many gifts that other fundraisers and volunteers solicit. They will see you as a resource to help them increase their effectiveness as fundraisers. But if you close yourself off and try to have exclusive "gift planning" prospects, you'll find yourself searching for prospects and the opportunity to do your job. All of the significant gifts we have ever worked on have involved others on the development team and from the nonprofit.

Training and Continuing Education

To be a successful gift planner, you will always be learning and growing. As you cultivate more donor relationships, you'll be asked to work on gifts that become more complex. Between us, we have over forty-five years of gift, estate and financial planning experience, yet we actively participate in continuing education programs offered by PPP, AFP, CASE (*case.org*), and AHP (*ahp.org*), as well as others. We also offer direct training in our methodology. These education sessions will help you continue to build your skill set over time and are vital to your professional growth and collaboration with colleagues.

To Recap

◆ One-on-one visits are the best way to build donor relationships that lead to planned gifts.

◆ Write and record a donor strategy for each assigned prospect from your identified, segmented list.

◆ Have a process to obtain and execute qualifying visits.

◆ It may take many cultivation visits before you can make a solicitation, but be sure each one is purposeful and moves the relationship forward.

◆ As your cultivation becomes more sophisticated, you will need to build your skill set to be able to meet the needs of your donors.

Chapter Eleven

Soliciting Prospects

In This Chapter

···→ Blended gifts

···→ Preparation

···→ Solicitation visits

···→ Negotiating the gift

You have built a relationship with the donor, understand the passions that tie the donor to your nonprofit, and explored personal planning objectives that may stand in the way of the donor making a gift. The donor is now ready, and likely expecting, you to start the gift planning conversation.

Blended Gifts

In the gift planning model, particularly as you work with New Philanthropists, you should not be thinking about making a transactional "ask." In that approach, you meet with a donor, determine capacity, find an area of interest at the nonprofit, and then ask for a gift at the nonprofit's estimate of the donor's capacity to the area of identified interest. If the donor says no, you ask if it was the project or the amount and adjust accordingly in the hopes of closing some type of gift.

Using a gift planning model, it will be clear when it is time to approach donors about gifts. You will have provided opportunities to fulfill passions through participation with the charity, and donors will be ready to do more. You will have inquired about what stands in the way of donors making commitments to bring their vision to reality. You will have explored solutions with donors and their advisors that help them meet all their goals—personal and philanthropic.

For most significant gift planning conversations with New Philanthropists (called philanthropic planning in *The Philanthropic Planning Companion*), your donors will want to continue (and typically increase) their annual support because they are engaging more fully in the mission, include multiyear major commitments to achieve philanthropic goals from which they can see immediate results, and add planned gifts to permanently endow the programs that have touched them. These are the donors you have cultivated who are making long-term, strategic investments in your mission. If you allow gifts to develop, they will provide everything you need to support your nonprofit today, five years from now, and permanently, as the donors will want to ensure their gifts achieve the desired results.

Not all gift planning conversations will be at this level. You will work with donors who are not ready to make this type of comprehensive investment in your mission. For some, the planned gift will be their first major commitment. It is a way for them to make larger gifts and test how your organization treats them. It might take the form of a $10,000 gift annuity or a will beneficiary designation with no value attached. If you treat them well, these relationships can mature over time and lead to philanthropic planning discussions that will meet your short, intermediate, and long-term funding goals. But if you try to force these conversations into the transactional model, you will lose the opportunity to bring these donors to the next level.

> ### Let the Gift Develop Organically
>
> We have shared that most gift planning donors are consistent annual fund donors who do not see themselves as major gift prospects. Now that you are ready to open a gift planning solicitation, do not fall into the trap of making the "combined ask" for an annual, major, and planned gift. The combined ask makes sense in a traditional, transactional fundraising shop. But in the world of the New Philanthropists, this won't work. Instead, focus on what your donors want to accomplish for themselves, their families, and your nonprofit, and let the gift develop organically.
>
>  **stories from the real world**

Preparation

Your donor should never be surprised when you ask for a gift. The work you have done in cultivation should make it clear that you are hoping that the donor will invest in the cause and that the series of cultivation visits is leading to that end.

Pre-Solicitation Visit

We suggest that you test your assumptions about your donor's intentions prior to the meeting when you actually have a gift discussion. During this visit, you reaffirm your understanding of the donor's passions, the particular area the donor seems inclined to support, and the estimated gift amount. By asking questions about these topics on a pre-solicitation visit, it allows the donor to get used to the idea of a gift and for you to gauge reactions to the purpose and amount. By the end of this meeting, the donor should be anticipating the formal gift conversation at the next visit.

Who Should Participate in the Solicitation Visit?

In the traditional transactional fundraising model, the head of the organization or a board member makes most of the high-end asks. In the philanthropic planning model, if you build the relationship, you should be the one having the gift conversation. Ideally you will have involved several other people from your organization in the cultivation process. The ones associated with the particular area of donor interest would accompany

> ### Show Your Donor Results
>
> As we have discussed regarding stewardship, sharing outcomes about how donors are truly supporting the mission will be your best encouragement toward additional gifts. The fully engaged donor who sees results through participation with your organization is going to be the most generous donor.
>
> **practical tip**

you to the solicitation meeting. They can add background information about the project and help overcome any objections to the purpose of the gift. For your Traditionalists, bring the CEO or a board member. They like to have the person in charge or with decision-making authority present. The New Philanthropists, particularly the Trailing Boomers, Gen Xers, and Millennials, would rather have the people involved in the project at the table.

When assembling a solicitation team, keep in mind that more than three people will seem like you are ganging up on the prospect. A team of two is usually best—you plus the person most closely tied to the project. A larger team becomes unwieldy and often will negatively impact the flow of the conversation or fill empty spaces, which are vital to the success of your gift discussion. Working in a team of two allows you to play off each other's strengths, with each of you speaking and listening as appropriate.

Anyone Can Make a Meaningful Gift

In my first job as a fundraiser, I worked for Clarkson University in Potsdam, New York. While there, I had the opportunity to meet a wonderful woman who had helped maintain one of the buildings on campus forever. She probably never made more than $15,000 per year. A few years after I left, I heard from my successor that she had passed on, leaving her entire estate, over $40,000, to the university to start an endowment to maintain the building she had cleaned for all those years. It was a powerful reminder that anyone connected to the mission can make a meaningful planned gift, no matter their apparent means.

—Brian

 stories from the real world

Scripting and Rehearsing the Solicitation

In the transactional model, it has become standard practice to script and rehearse the ask. With untrained fundraisers, particularly the CEO and board members, having these conversations and scripts help guide the conversation, anticipate objections, and keep the conversation on track. Without a script, these meetings can get off track and frequently the ask would never be made.

In the gift planning model, there should not be a need for a script. The team having the solicitation conversation should absolutely meet ahead of time to plan a strategy for the conversation, but it is a different conversation from the transactional ask. You should already know what the donor is passionate

An Unorthodox Strategy for Completing the Gift Discussion

I use an unorthodox strategy for completing the gift discussion. Rather than ask for a particular amount, I typically will offer to the donor the total cost of the project and ask the donor to be a lead supporter on the project. This allows the donor to give me a number with which the donor is comfortable. If it is lower than my ideal number, I will share it and explain why a gift at that number is important to help the donor meet the philanthropic goal of seeing this project completed. If the donor's number is higher, I have avoided leaving money on the table.

We then discuss how to structure the gift, including annual, current, and planned giving options, and even what assets make sense to complete the commitment. Sometimes the conversation about how to structure the gift allows us to reach the number the nonprofit needs to complete the project. But by focusing on the mission first, completing the rest of the gift conversation is a relatively easy task.

—Brian

 practical tip

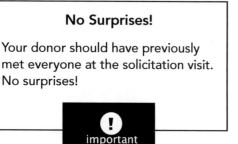

No Surprises!

Your donor should have previously met everyone at the solicitation visit. No surprises!

important

about and have educated the donor how you are pursuing, or planning to pursue, that area of the cause. It will result in an organic conversation that has come from months and sometimes years of cultivation and has been revisited several times before the solicitation meeting. This usually means that there is no formal "proposal" to be presented to the donor at the meeting. This proposal will be replaced by a discussion of the terms of the gift agreement in the negotiation process.

Solicitation Visits

Having done so much to prepare your donor for the solicitation visit, the actual conversation may seem anticlimactic.

If the donor raises objections to the project, you may not have fully explored the donor's passions and interests in the cultivation process. You need to immediately take a step back and reevaluate. It is certainly not the time to ask what else interests the donor and try to gain a gift commitment to an alternate area.

If the donor raises concerns about the amount, you should first appeal to the donor's passion for the project, then begin to explore personal-planning issues that may stand in the way of completing the gift or asset-selection issues that may help overcome any cash-flow issues. Most donors still think about giving from their incomes, not from their assets. If you can suggest alternative "pockets" from which to draw philanthropic support (e.g., gifts of stock, business interests, overfunded retirement accounts, and no-longer-needed life insurance policies) and can offer to work with a donor's advisors, you are much more likely to find a solution that results in the kind of gift your donor wants to make.

At the close of the meeting, summarize the conversation and next steps for you and for your donor. Assuming that the donor wants to go forward but needs time to consider what has been proposed, the next step is to negotiate the details of the gift.

We often use the following language, which we introduced in *The Philanthropic Planning Companion:*

We have been talking about _____ for several months, which is clearly very important to you. Together, we believe we can help you to realize your goal of _____ for those served by our charity. The last time we met, we discussed your support for this area and how we could partner together to make your vision a reality. The total cost to complete this project is going to be $_____. Where would you see yourself in making this happen?

Example

Negotiating the Gift

By far the most overlooked and poorly executed part of the gift planning process is the negotiation of the gift. Organizations tend to put so much emphasis and importance on the solicitation that once it is complete, they are not at all ready to negotiate the gift and commit the understanding to writing.

A well-crafted gift agreement will document the gift, establishing what the charity has agreed to, what the donor has agreed to, the assets to be used to make the gift, the gift structure, and how the gift will be recognized and stewarded. It ensures that the donor's wishes are carried out and helps propel the relationship forward.

You should provide the donor and the advisors with a draft gift agreement within forty-eight hours of the solicitation visit. Advisors play a key role in ensuring the gift agreement meets the personal planning needs of the donor. There is more information, including a sample gift agreement, in Chapter Six of the *Resource Book.*

It may take one or more negotiation visits with the donor and advisors to complete the gift agreement. When all of the details have been ironed out, the final gift agreement is executed by the donor and your nonprofit. Then the real joy of philanthropy can begin—turning the gift into meaningful impact and outcomes for your nonprofit.

To Recap

◆ The gift planning model is not focused on the ask but on helping a donor invest in the cause while meeting personal planning objectives.

◆ Gift planning conversations with high-end donors require a philanthropic planning approach, which will frequently result in a gift with annual, major, and planned gift components.

◆ Even donors without major capacity can make significant planned gifts.

◆ Careful preparation through a pre-solicitation visit to test assumptions about capacity and interest, as well as a thorough solicitation strategy, will produce better results.

◆ No surprises at the solicitation visit.

◆ Negotiating the gift agreement gives you an opportunity to revisit solicitation discussions that did not go well.

◆ A well-thought-out gift agreement will ensure that the goals of the donor and your nonprofit are documented and carried out.

Chapter Twelve

Concierge Stewardship

In This Chapter

---→ Tell your story

---→ Remind your donors of the outcomes of their past giving

---→ The role of seven touches in stewardship

---→ Core elements to include in your gift planning stewardship program

Stewardship is the art of managing the relationships between donors and your organization. A successful stewardship program will increase your connection with your gift planning supporters, causing them to become more engaged with your mission and desiring to help fund vital programs that further your success. In fact, successful, mature gift planning programs receive up to 50 percent of their new life-income gifts from existing life-income gift donors who feel well connected and stewarded by the organization. Stewardship requires proper acknowledgment of donations of time, talent, and treasure, the three legs of donor participation.

An effective thank-you, recognition, and stewardship program will produce donors who feel appreciated and respected. They will be more engaged by your mission, making them more likely to direct gifts to meet organizational needs and priorities. Over time, this increased level of engagement should lead to larger outright gifts and additional planned gifts.

Well-stewarded donors will eventually look for a wider range of charitable-giving tools to integrate their philanthropic goals for all of the organizations they support with their tax, estate, and financial planning. They will become shareholders and engage others to support those charitable missions, becoming your best ambassadors.

> **The Art of Stewardship**
>
> *Stewardship is the art of making someone who has just made a small gift wish that they might have made your organization a bigger one.*
>
> —Robert
>
> " "

Take Time to Write Your Organization's Story

Mark Twain, like many writers, felt that it was often easier to write at length than to create something short and succinct. He once received a telegram from his publisher that read: "NEED 2-PAGE SHORT STORY TWO DAYS."

Twain sent the following reply: "NO CAN DO 2 PAGES 2 DAYS. CAN DO 30 PAGES 2 DAYS. NEED 30 DAYS TO DO 2 PAGES."

Tell Your Story

Effective stewardship actually starts with a well-written story that reflects the essence of your nonprofit's mission. After all, whether it is an outright gift or a planned gift, prospects give to support your mission.

Take time to write your organization's story. Share the passion that motivates you to work for your organization, and that should motivate others to give.

You need a story that can evoke a response from your audience that brings out its passion for the mission of your organization. And, fortunately, you probably represent an organization that has a powerful mission statement, the kind of organization that continues to offer outcomes that excite your donors and cause repeat giving.

With a good story in place about your mission and the outcomes created by past gifts in support of it, you next must focus your attention on the donors who continue to provide for the future as you cherish their support. We have all drunk from wells we did not dig, been warmed by fires we did not build, and sat in the shade of trees we did not plant. Do not forget your donors, many of whom have worked hard for the money they invest in your organization.

When building a stewardship effort, you start with your annual donors, as they will eventually become your gift planning prospects. Fifty percent of first-time donors never make a second gift to the same nonprofit organization. Why is donor retention so poor? When surveyed, donors say it is a failure to thank, recognize, and steward. And when you consider that planned gifts are developed from loyal donors, it can provide for a bleak outlook for future gift planning opportunities. Nonprofits lose on average 30 percent of their overall donor pool each year. William T. Sturtevant stated in his book *The*

Do Our Donors Share Our Story?

Do we encourage our donors to share our story with others? Are they so engaged that they want to tell their friends about what is being accomplished with their help? Or do we try to keep our donors by "clipping their wings?" On a trip to England, I visited the Tower of London and saw the famous guards and the crown jewels as well as the ravens that, according to myth, will cause the British throne to fall if they leave. Not surprisingly, the British government clips the ravens' wings to prevent them from flying away. We recently adopted a leadership case for support that has several responsibilities for our trustees, including sharing our story as ambassadors in the community. One of our newest board members and most generous donors has taken his role seriously and has been telling the story to appropriate individuals, including a business owner who has now agreed to make his own significant gift and perhaps join our board. Not only is the organization encouraging our volunteers to share the story, but the very experience of doing so is providing stewardship to our donor.

—Robert

stories from the real world

Artful Journey that "it requires four-and-a-half times the effort, staff, and dollars to acquire a new donor as it does to keep one." A nonprofit's best effort is, therefore, spent maintaining and even building current relationships with donors.

Nonprofits spend an enormous sum each year trying to lure back lapsed donors and identify new prospects. Yet they consistently send the message to their modest annual fund donors that their gifts of time, money, and effort are not important.

If nonprofits spent a small portion of their donor-acquisition budgets on meaningful thank you notes, they would retain a much larger percentage of their annual donors, turn them into loyal donors, and eventually convert them to planned gift donors. As Penelope Burk shares in her book *Donor-Centered Fundraising*: "On a gift-by-gift basis, budgeting communication and recognition relative to gift size seems to make sense, but it is actually the *opposite* of what we need to do if we want to retain more donors and increase the average value of contributions. We make the mistake of designing and budgeting communication as a post-gift activity instead of what it really is—the investment cost of securing the next gift."

The Meeting with My Children Started Well, and Went Downhill from There

Over the last ten years, my wife and I have been making an effort to teach our children about philanthropy, using some great ideas from Carol Weisman's book *Raising Charitable Children*. In 2012, two of our children (aged sixteen and fourteen) chose a new nonprofit to support, one focused on Hurricane Sandy relief.

Things started well but quickly went downhill. I called the nonprofit and asked if we could come and see them, explaining that we were teaching our kids about philanthropy. The charity graciously agreed to send a representative to the house. He was a kind gentleman who proceeded to explain to my children that hurricane relief was "oversubscribed" and suggested that they direct their gift to overall disaster relief. After some prodding, my disappointed children eventually agreed and wrote a check for $450 to support the cause, an awful lot for children their ages to have earned and saved for a charitable purpose. It was December 21.

January and February 2013 came and went without a word from the charity. In early March, two formal letters (dated February 7) arrived from the nonprofit, each with a salutation to "Ms. Sagrestano." These very formal form letters were identical, except for the name in the address line at the top. They talked about "this hurricane season," which of course by March had been over for months. At the bottom, it used a scanned signature from a regional executive the kids did not know and had never met. My younger daughter opened the letter, read it intently, and then tossed it in the recycling. I asked her why she was throwing it out, and she said, "Clearly, my gift was not important to them."

The nonprofit had started so well, sending a representative to the house. But then that representative told my daughters they could not direct their gift as intended, the organization took nearly three months to acknowledge the gift, and the letters acknowledging the gift were out of date, not truly personalized, and not appropriate to the donors who made the gifts.

My children have already informed me that they will not donate to this very worthy organization ever again. This can be a valuable lesson for us all—follow the platinum rule of fundraising—treat donors as they want to be treated—especially first-time annual donors.

—Brian

 stories from the real world

You may be wondering why we are spending so much time on outright gift stewardship in a book on charitable gift planning. When you consider that the vast majority of planned gifts come from individuals who are regular, consistent donors, you understand that without a strong stewardship effort of annual giving donors, there are no gift planning prospects. So when you build your gift planning stewardship effort, it starts with your annual donors.

Remind Your Donors of the Outcomes of Their Past Giving

Not all outcomes are as you expect. In his will, Shakespeare left his wife his "second best bed." We are not sure what that really means, but no doubt it was a surprise.

Higher education does well to remind its alums of the success of their giving by telling about the success of their many graduates and offering tours of new buildings and facilities during reunion weekends. Health systems can boast of new equipment in new units or expanded hospital pavilions. A new performance can bring the applause of donors who see what their memberships bring to a theater. By sharing outcomes created by past gifts, you confirm to your donors that their giving is important, makes a difference, and will continue to have an impact long after they have passed on. This approach creates the type of loyalty that makes a gift planning program thrive.

Whether they are multimillionaires or donors of modest means, each donor seeks to make a gift with a purpose. The purpose can be exactly the same for each of these populations—fulfilling human potential, as an example. The wealthy might then think about setting up a foundation to fulfill this purpose on a large scale like Bill and Melinda Gates have done, while a more modest donor might look to help one hungry child through individual sponsorship. When we practice proper stewardship, giving by either means should offer the same outcome of fulfilling the human potential of the donors. For multimillionaires, it might be the realization that they can make a significant difference in a way that is superior to their daily routines with their businesses. For others, it might be the realization that although they cannot afford much, they are making a difference for one child and doing their part. In either case, the outcome of their giving is meaningful to them and their beneficiaries.

Offer Meaningful Volunteer Opportunities

In days past, stewardship of planned giving donors involved a simple thank-you lunch once per year. Today, donors seek volunteer opportunities to bring to life the financial commitments they have made. Those donors who are most engaged with your mission are the best prospects for gift planning. Once they set up planned gifts, they become even more engaged and want to do even more financially and personally.

The Traditionalists (born pre-1946) welcome the volunteer opportunities that have become

---

We Feel the Outcome of Our Giving

My coauthor and I are proud Eagle Scouts, and while my son recently became a Boy Scout, Brian and I have spent several years of our adult lives as Scouting volunteers. The values that are developed through the program are enhanced with every activity. We have witnessed boys helping physically challenged boys have the same experience. We have heard young men lead other boys through physically and mentally challenging outdoor experiences. We have both recited the Scout Oath and Law for more than thirty years of our lives and still join in when we hear young Scouts raise their right hands and repeat it today. Our past and current giving is rewarded every time we participate in a Scouting activity. Whether a camping or canoe trip, a hike, or a parade, we feel the outcome of our giving.

—Robert

 **stories from the real world**

the norm in charitable giving circles. Serving on boards or advisory committees, attending awareness-raising events, handwriting invitations, and making phone calls are all good ways to engage Traditionalists.

Leading Boomers (born 1946–1954) will still serve in many of these traditional roles, but they find them less interesting than the Traditionalists. They are looking for more leisure time, particularly after working so hard for so many years. If the activities involve their children, they may have a greater interest in participating, particularly if they can show adult or teenaged children that they are helping pursue the social justice agenda of their youth.

> ### Habitat for Humanity
>
> Habitat for Humanity does a tremendous job in giving its donors an experience so they truly understand the outcome of their giving. Not only do its donors write a check, but then they can participate in the construction of the house that will change someone's life.
>
> **Example**

Trailing Boomers (born 1955–1964) are much less interested in traditional volunteer roles. Instead, they want to volunteer time in areas that their planned gift will eventually support. For example, if a Trailing Boomer makes a gift in support of bringing the arts to inner-city schools, the volunteer opportunity should be to help create and promote the concert for those benefitting from the program.

Gen X (born 1965–1975) wants nothing to do with traditional stewardship events or volunteer opportunities. This generation will give and volunteer only to causes that touch them personally. Volunteer opportunities need to allow them to be creative to help solve a problem that is of interest to them.

Millennials (born 1977–1984) are full of positive energy and fresh ideas, and they are plugged in. Nonprofits that give Millennials responsibility for meaningful volunteer activities will find that the Millennials will come up with creative new ways to achieve the goals of the nonprofit while engaging other Millennials. While most gift planning programs will not have a lot of Millennial donors until they get a bit older, those who can be engaged at this stage of life will be a welcome addition and will draw in others.

The Role of Seven Touches in Stewardship

Nonprofits need to appropriately recognize all of their donors, even those who wish to remain anonymous. Giving may be its own reward, but a thoughtfully conceived, donor-focused recognition program is indispensable to the success of any philanthropic program.

Donor recognition has a twofold purpose: to thank donors for their gifts and to encourage donors (and others) to upgrade their gifts. Recognition begins at

> ### Experiencing the Outcome for Myself
>
> Rebuilding Together provides critical repairs and renovations for low-income homeowners across the United States and has done so for almost twenty-five years. I was fortunate to have an experience over two days with this amazing organization in the hardest-hit Ninth Ward of New Orleans following the devastation of Hurricane Katrina. In giving my time, my talent, and my treasure, I felt fulfilled when meeting the elderly couple whose home we were repairing. They were so appreciative, and that was all the outcome I needed to see.
>
> —Robert
>
>  **stories from the real world**

the moment that the donor makes the commitment. The initial sincere response lets donors know how thrilled the organization is to have them join in support of the cause.

Jerold Panas in *Mega Gifts* recommends finding a way to thank donors seven times each year. Seven distinct moves offer seven opportunities for donors to understand that they are important to your nonprofit. Seven messages that are singular but when positioned together work toward a complete concept of reminding donors both why they are giving and what their support is accomplishing.

Core Elements to Include in Your Gift Planning Stewardship Effort

Up to this point, we have shared with you a different way to steward your gift planning donors. We started by suggesting that you tell your story to reaffirm your donors' ties to your mission. We then encouraged you to tell great outcomes-based stories, highlighting past gifts. These stories make the connection between your mission and philanthropic support. We then directed you to create meaningful volunteer opportunities that will engage gift planning donors in the life of your nonprofit going forward, to bring the outcomes to life. Just as important, these opportunities must be tailored by generational cohorts, as each generation is looking for different types of experiences. Finally, we suggested that each gift planning donor should be targeted with seven meaningful forms of thank-you each year.

Memories of Our Past Can Become Building Blocks for Today

In building a program that will thrive, remember that the memories of our past can become the building blocks for today . . . and tomorrow. In looking around my office, I realized that all of the photos and mementos I had accumulated represented the past. I considered removing them and starting anew as I wanted to organize the clutter and be more focused in my workplace, but I wondered if those reminders of people, places, and events might serve some purpose beyond nostalgia. To avoid being too mired in the "yesterdays" of life, I needed to discover the value of those items for today and tomorrow. They, in fact, inspire me to continue to create good memories.

I am fortunate to have met Linda about two years ago, as she called to speak with me after the death of her father, one of the talented surgeons who had built Jersey Shore University Medical Center into the hospital that it is today. She told me about her dad and her family and all the good times they had while they also dealt with all that life throws at us. After several conversations and two visits, she decided to make a gift to honor him and the work he did.

As we planned the dedication ceremony, we reviewed a collection of photos that she had assembled. At first, they all seemed to be disjointed, but as we worked together to put them in order, it was clear to me that, together, they told a poignant story about a man who helped others and exemplified the idea of living life to its fullest.

I then had the chance to meet one of Linda's sons, and she told me over lunch how her two sons had just created a business that actively encourages people to have the best day of their life. We talked about how people would wear T-shirts that say "The Best Day of My Life" while they enjoyed something they loved. They would then be able to post their pictures on Facebook and through other social media outlets to create the excitement of sharing their positive experiences. We talked about our best days, and we concluded that the idea would be uplifting in that you might look forward to the "tomorrows" in your life as you continually tried to have a better day than today.

—Robert

observation

To help you implement these strategies, we have included practical materials and advice in the accompanying *Resource Book.* From reconfigured legacy societies to updated print materials, these tools will help you as you steward this audience.

To truly offer a donor-focused approach, the examples we provide in the *Resource Book* should be amended to match the constituents of your particular organization. The meter of the approach is proven, but the touches should be tailored to the donors and the mission.

Concierge Stewardship

In *The Philanthropic Planning Companion*, we introduced the concept of "Concierge Stewardship" for high-net-worth donors. Just like stewardship of gift planning donors, high-net-worth philanthropists need to feel a lifetime of commitment to and from the charity. The difference is in the delivery of stewardship activities. Throughout the philanthropic planning process, this group of donors was worthy of one-on-one attention, and their stewardship should be no different. In addition to the methods described, organizations should offer stewardship that is personal and customized to their needs and objectives, or "concierge stewardship."

Unlike the approach for annual giving and gift planning, concierge stewardship gives donors exactly what they have stated they want to see from the organization in their stewardship. A very creative and, again, customized program is mapped out to provide the philanthropist with the seven touches that will remind them that they are valuable to the organization.

Like the concierge service at a fine hotel, the organization might offer a menu of items it can provide for a donor. Organizations will have distinctly different offerings that are chosen by the fundraiser, as the primary relationship manager for the organization, and are picked based on the fundraiser's knowledge of the donors and their wishes. This approach gives donors a very tailored stewardship regimen.

For example, with a chance to show the outcomes of their giving, an organization might engage donors in experiences that would give them a firsthand look. In health care, an opportunity to shadow a physician for an afternoon for rounds. Or in higher education, an invitation to attend a lecture on a topic interesting to donors in an area that was funded by them would offer tremendous glimpses into the program that is a result of their generosity.

Concierge stewardship ensures that philanthropists are receiving the attention, information, and experiences they expect as investors in the organization's mission.

To Recap

- Effective stewardship starts by tying your donors to your mission.

- Stewardship of every donor is important to your organization.

- Stewardship of new and loyal donors will increase their commitment to the cause.

- Telling outcomes-based stories cements the connection between philanthropy and results.

- Volunteer opportunities bring outcomes to life.

- A strong stewardship program will include at least seven touches with each of your donors annually.

- For high-net-worth donors, concierge stewardship will offer a strong return on the philanthropic investment.

Part Four

Marketing Gift Planning

I n **Part Three**, we discussed how you identify and approach gift planning prospects one on one. Unfortunately, you likely won't have enough time or staff resources to visit all of your identified gift planning prospects, which is the best way to close planned gifts. In **Part Four**, we discuss how you can build a marketing plan on a moves management platform to reach identified gift planning prospects as well as other individuals interested in your mission, but not among the loyals group.

Chapter Thirteen

Marketing in a Donor-focused Way

In This Chapter

---→ The role of marketing in gift planning

---→ The four tiers of the gift planning marketing pyramid

---→ Build your marketing plan around your most loyal donors

---→ Integrating gift planning marketing into your moves management process

For years, gift planning marketing was the same approach year after year: Send a large number of newsletters describing some gift planning technique to old, wealthy prospects in your database and hope that some of them would respond. The newsletter would include a nice profile of an older couple who had completed a gift, explaining why they chose to support the charity and giving details of the particular gift vehicle in context. The newsletter also included information about the nonprofit's legacy society, often with photos of its most recent luncheon.

Unfortunately, these newsletters began to lose their efficacy in the early 2000s as donors became overwhelmed, receiving the same type of newsletter communication from several nonprofits they supported. The explosion of newsletters coincided with the 1999 release of a study by Paul D. Schervish and John J. Havens titled *Millionaires and the Millennium: New Estimates of the Forthcoming Wealth Transfer and the Prospects for a Golden Age in Philanthropy* detailing a $41 trillion transfer of wealth, of which $6 trillion to $7 trillion would come to nonprofits between 1998 and 2052. So why, if there was to be this tremendous transfer of wealth, was gift planning marketing suddenly proving so ineffective?

There were two main causes: First, the newsletters were trying to do too much. They were educating, cultivating, soliciting, and stewarding in a single mailing. The majority of the newsletters simply weren't read. And when prospects were surveyed, they didn't even remember receiving them.

Second, at this same time, the Traditionalists (born pre-1946) were passing the age of sixty in droves, the age at which recent studies tell us they become less likely to alter their estate plans to include new nonprofits for which they do not have an affinity. So ineffective marketing coupled with changing donor demographics caused gift planning marketing to lose effectiveness at the moment when charities needed it the most.

The Role of Marketing in Gift Planning

To address these marketing challenges, Brian developed a new model based on a different gift planning marketing pyramid and built on a moves management platform. The core idea is that the best gift planning is done one-on-one with identified prospects at the top of the pyramid—but that the best gift planning *marketing* is done with the identified prospects in the "loyals" tier of the pyramid. You then include gift planning marketing across your existing multichannel marketing platform to introduce gift planning to "everyone else" in case they might be interested. By doing so through your existing marketing, there is little to no cost to reach this bottom level of prospect.

Four Tiers of the Gift Planning Marketing Pyramid

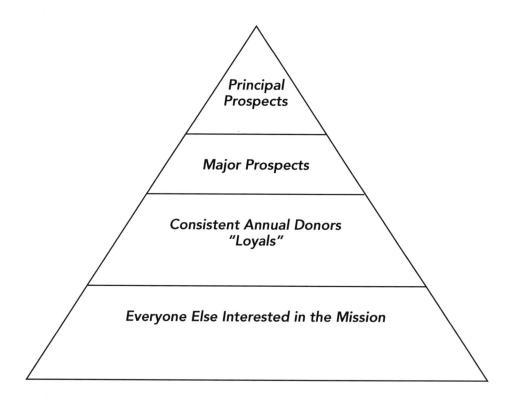

We first introduced the gift planning marketing pyramid in *The Philanthropic Planning Companion*. The top two tiers, principal and major prospects, are the individuals you approach one-on-one as outlined in **Part Three**. The loyals are the target for the vast majority of your gift planning marketing efforts. When they express interest, you visit with them to move through a gift planning process. If anyone from "everyone else" responds to your materials in the existing multichannel marketing effort, you treat them the same way.

Integrating Gift Planning Marketing into Your Moves Management Process

The first step in building your gift planning marketing program is to create your list as described in **Chapter Nine**. Remember that you always start by determining your loyal prospects. Only after you have that list do you start to segment the list. You can segment by wealth, generational cohorts, gender, and a wide range of other variables. But if a prospect is not loyal, there is no point in pursuing a planned gift.

With the list in place, you then need to overlay your gift planning marketing strategy onto your existing moves management platform. If you do not have a moves management system, you need to create one, as outlined in **Chapter Ten**. Moves management is much like a sales cycle for fundraising. It sets a timeline and process that guides you in your identification of potential prospects, education of identified prospects about your mission, cultivation of a relationship between the prospect and your nonprofit, pre-solicitation of a gift where you test the prospect's interest, the actual solicitation, negotiation of the terms of the gift, and stewardship of the relationship after the gift is completed or the commitment is made.

Over time, a well-defined gift planning marketing plan will help propel prospects through your moves management process. Most gift planning marketing efforts consist of "random acts of marketing." There is no system or plan. The nonprofit just sends something out every once in a while, depending upon who is staffing the gift planning program or the vendor they have selected for gift planning purposes. Unfortunately, this type of program has little chance for success because there is no thought as to how the piece or activity moves the gift planning effort forward, and there frequently is no tracking of the success of the effort.

In the moves management context, each marketing touch has a clearly defined purpose, content, audience, schedule, budget, and measures of success. Most importantly, each touch is designed to fit with one step in the moves management process. This way, you are moving an identified group of prospects from the education phase right to the ask over a set period of time.

Over the next three chapters, we will share with you different tools and techniques for building and executing your donor-focused gift planning marketing plan on a moves management platform. We will also introduce our marketing grid, which is a simple, one-page spreadsheet that will assist you as you build your program.

To Recap

◆ One-on-one meetings are the best way to close planned gifts, not gift planning marketing.

"Plannual Giving"

Loyal annual donors can be the best prospects for planned gifts. Consider a "plannual giving" approach in your gift planning marketing efforts by working closely with annual giving. By adding messaging about gift planning and a check box on the reply card for those who have remembered their favorite Meridian hospital in their will or estate plan, we are already seeing a return on our investment with twenty gifts totaling more than $15,000. Direct mail that cultivates gifts that lead to loyal annual donors provides a great opportunity to add to your plan to grow planned gifts.

—Robert

 stories from the real world

---

When Less is More

When I arrived at the University of Pennsylvania, the university's gift planning marketing program was largely ineffective. Working with Colleen Elisii, associate director of gift planning marketing, we scrapped our 36,000-piece traditional gift planning newsletter. We turned it into a stewardship piece mailed to 3,600 people that focused on their need to stay connected to the university. Even though we were mailing to 90 percent fewer people, the 3,600-piece mailing received almost exactly the same total number of responses as the 36,000-piece mailing. We then found other ways to reach our broader population in existing publications at a far lower cost.

—Brian

 stories from the real world

◆ Traditional gift planning marketing is no longer effective due to changing donor demographics and the proliferation of canned gift planning materials that try to do too much.

◆ Targeted marketing to identified gift planning prospects on a moves management platform has the highest likelihood of success.

Chapter Fourteen

Marketing to Everyone

In This Chapter

---→ "What, no gift planning vehicles?"

---→ Meeting personal planning objectives

---→ Tools of Marketing

---→ Marketing grid

When building your gift planning marketing strategy, you should build from the top of the gift planning marketing pyramid down, since the prospects at the top have the highest capacity and inclination to make planned gifts. So you may be wondering why we are starting from the bottom in providing you with gift planning marketing tools. Because both are equally important.

You will certainly want to approach the prospects at the top of the pyramid personally and perhaps may use a bit of marketing. You will then target the loyals and cultivate them regularly, with some of them moving up the pyramid as you learn more about them. Potential prospects from "everyone else" will eventually join your loyals, and some of them will also move up the pyramid. But if you do not build the bottom of the pyramid, eventually the well of prospects will run dry.

"What, No Gift Planning Vehicles?"

Before we start describing particular marketing tools to use with everyone else, we need to address some common misconceptions about gift planning. Gift planning is not about the tools or vehicles used to help prospects complete planned gifts. As we outlined in **Part One**, gift planning is about helping prospects integrate their philanthropy into their overall tax, estate, and financial planning. The vehicles are just a means to that end.

This may well be a new concept for you, as for years nonprofits did exactly that: market the tools, vehicles, and tax savings. "Buy a gift annuity with XYZ charity," "Learn the benefits of the wonderful charitable remainder trust," and "Avoid estate taxes through a charitable bequest."

Reach All Levels of the Gift Planning Pyramid

Your gift planning marketing plan must reach individuals at all levels of the gift planning pyramid. Each level supports the level above it. If you build only the top, you do not have a secure foundation of future prospects and the pyramid will fail. The entire structure is required for success.

important

This approach worked with transactional donors who trusted charities to do the right thing. They were buying a product from the charity to help a cause they believed in. These were the Traditionalists (born pre-1946), and most fundraising and gift planning programs were built to appeal to them. But when the Traditionalists passed their peak earning and giving years and nonprofits began to solicit the Leading Boomers (born 1946–1954) for planned gifts, these strategies lost effectiveness and needed to be replaced with strategies targeted at these up-and-coming generational cohorts.

Meeting Personal Planning Objectives

For the New Philanthropists (born 1946-present), the model requires you to help them meet personal planning objectives with their philanthropy in an integrated way. This notion stems from two different circumstances. First, the New Philanthropists do not trust nonprofits the way that Traditionalists did. This means that while a Traditionalist was happy to take your advice about the benefits of a gift annuity, charitable remainder trust or bequest, the New Philanthropists want to check with their advisors. As outlined in *The Philanthropic Planning Companion*, very few New Philanthropists consider nonprofits as a trustworthy source of information about charitable gift planning.

Second, the New Philanthropists simply do not have the same sources of income in retirement as their predecessors. Traditionalists were savers who lived through times of struggle and difficulty in the Great Depression and World War II. Even though they didn't earn a great deal, they saved what they could for fear of another bad economic downturn. They also worked in a world of pensions, so many of them already had secure income for retirement provided by their companies. As a result, Traditionalists are fairly secure in their retirement. As they have aged, they have been able to make gifts from their nonretirement assets according to their means or, more likely, through their estates to

The World of Gift Planning Has Changed

During the recent recession, one of my clients had just built a donor-focused gift planning marketing program. The organization was getting good early responses, but management started pressuring the gift planning staff to "close gifts." (I know this never happens to you!) The vice president of development directed the gift planner to produce a postcard and mail it to the broadest audience possible of wealthy people over the age of sixty-five, stating, "In these difficult economic times, isn't it good to know that you rely on the stable income provided by a gift annuity with XYZ Charity?"

I recognized the piece, as I had developed something very similar during the dot.com bust and gotten great results with it. However, due to the changes in donor demographics since 2001 and the sheer cost of this kind of marketing, I strongly encouraged the organization not to develop and send it. As sometimes happens, the consultant lost out to the vice president. The nonprofit mailed 11,000 pieces and got two responses, resulting in no new gifts. It was yet another reminder that the world of gift planning marketing has indeed changed.

—Brian

stories from the real world

be sure that they didn't need the assets to maintain their standard of living.

The New Philanthropists are not so fortunate. The Leading Boomers were not savers, and now 60 percent of them are retiring (ten thousand every day) with no assets put away for retirement and with no pension. They will rely upon Social Security or an inheritance from their Traditionalist parents to support them in their later years. If they are to make charitable gifts, they will need those gifts to supplement their retirement income. The 40 percent who have saved may have less than they would like, and certainly are likely to spend more in retirement than their predecessors. This desire for assets will put a damper on charitable giving.

That "Annuity" or "Trust Thing"

Over our careers, we have had many donors approach us to talk about that "annuity" or that "trust thing," and no matter how much they may have read and heard about them, the tools and vehicles are just the start of the conversation. If marketing is done right, the mission of your organization will ignite the passion of the donors to encourage them to take action based on their interests and needs.

observation

The Trailing Boomers (born 1955–1964) spent their entire careers stuck behind the Leading Boomers, which depressed their earning potential. They have less saved for retirement and will be seeking gift planning solutions to help them fill this gap. They are also in many cases supporting elderly parents in addition to their own children, putting them in a real financial squeeze. The Trailing Boomers will need their gifts to be fully integrated into their other planning to meet current and future income needs.

Retirement savings for Generation X (born 1965–1976) were hit the hardest by the Great Recession. Overall savings were cut in half as the stock and housing markets collapsed. Couple that with Gen X's reduced earning power due to their work-life balance approach to careers and penchant to start their own businesses, and they will have less security in retirement than any generation before them. If they are to make planned gifts, they will need to be gifts that cost them nothing today or gifts that provide them with retirement support.

The Millennials (born 1977–1984) will fare little better. Their early work careers have been marked by a desire to change the world and collect experiences. This has resulted in start-stop work patterns where they work for a couple of years to earn enough money to go do something and then stop working to go live the experience. When the money runs out, they come back to work. This has resulted in very little saving and long-term thinking about retirement. If their philanthropy does not help them solve this challenge, they will not be able to give.

The Philanthropy of Leading Boomers

My parents are Leading Boomers in every sense of the word. They were not savers and, in fact, over the years have spent and enjoyed themselves while also providing for my brother and me. The timing of the bad economy did not help my parents. While they were able to retire as planned, they are using all their resources to support themselves. In addition, my mom is now the one who is taking care of her ninety-four-year-old mother, so they also have that additional burden to contend with in their lives. They continue to be generous but now are more so with their time and talent. Both of my parents regularly volunteer and help raise money since they are not able to make large gifts of assets themselves.

—Robert

 **stories from the real world**

Leading by Example

We are Gen Xers and examples of gift planners who have made planned gifts. Not only is this leading by example, but it also helps us meet personal planning objectives for our families while adding to the legacies we have created with organizations that have been meaningful to us over our lives. Remember: It is easier to ask for planned gifts if you have already made one (or more) yourself.

observation

The Boomerang or Great Recession generation (born 1985–present) is still emerging as a group. In fact, social scientists have not yet fully defined the end of the Millennials and the start of this next generation. What we do know is that their earning potential has been drastically reduced by the poor job market at the time they have been entering the workforce. It is unknown if they will ever recover from these lower earnings at the start of their careers, meaning their earning potential and retirement savings could also be negatively impacted.

With the New Philanthropists living in a world where they do not trust nonprofits and need to integrate their philanthropy into their overall planning, the face of gift planning marketing must change to meet these needs. The best messages to use when marketing to New Philanthropists are:

◆ increasing income when you retire

◆ increasing your current retirement income

◆ providing for your elderly parent(s) or loved one(s)

◆ paying for college for your children

◆ crafting a meaningful legacy

At the same time, you cannot stop marketing to the Traditionalists, who are most likely to respond to messages for:

◆ increasing your current retirement income

◆ maximizing your children or grandchildren's inheritance

◆ gifts that cost nothing today

◆ paying for college for your grandchildren

◆ crafting a meaningful legacy

As you can see, there is some overlap in the messaging, but they do largely respond to different messages. As you put together your gift planning marketing plan, you'll have to consider how to segment your messaging to the different cohorts. When it comes to marketing to everyone else, you'll need to market to all the cohorts in the various pieces you use, recognizing that certain cohorts may be more likely to look at certain media than others and message appropriately.

Existing Publications and e-Publications

To reach this broad audience of everyone else, the first step is to create a communications inventory of existing outreach. The inventory is a chronological list of all of the publications and outreach you send to those interested in your mission, including the type of piece, target audience, number sent, send dates, due date for submissions, individual responsible for content, and response mechanism. With the inventory in hand, it becomes a simple matter to evaluate each piece and determine how a gift planning message can be integrated into it. You then add that piece to your gift planning marketing grid in the appropriate moves management stage. Before you know it, you'll have a complete plan for everyone else.

Open the general magazine or regular newsletter for almost any nonprofit and you'll find an advertisement for gift planning. These organizations have learned to start the seven touches process with everyone else through broad dissemination of information in the marketing piece sent to their largest audience. Because this piece is already being designed and published, there is little actual cost to your nonprofit to add gift planning messaging.

Creating Meaningful Ads

To create meaningful ads for the general publication, first consider the audience members. Most general publications are targeted at the entire mailing list. Because the list is so broad, segmenting by generational cohorts, gender, or no kids makes little sense in this context. The message must appeal to all groups. In such cases, focus your ads on what motivates the vast majority of individuals to consider planned gifts. Several studies, including one by Sargeant and Shang, have shown us that, generally, people respond to these messages:

◆ Prestige

◆ Reciprocity

◆ Organizational performance, professionalism, communication quality, and program quality

◆ Family need

◆ Need to live on

◆ Making a difference

> **Using an Ad Journal**
>
> If your organization holds special events that utilize an ad journal to boost income, consider including an ad in each one that's consistent with your gift planning marketing for that quarter. Like annual giving efforts, special events often have consistent support from those donors who believe in your mission but may enjoy attending events. Your ad journal ad can complement the messages they see in your other efforts. I have used this idea at Meridian Health, the American Cancer Society, and the Boy Scouts of America and have been amazed how several people have mentioned it to start a conversation about their own interest in making a gift.
>
> —Robert
>
> 👍 practical tip

While there are many different ways to approach ads that use these motivating factors, the LEAVE A LEGACY ads produced by the Partnership for Philanthropic Planning encompass many of the best practices highlighted. View these sample ads at *leavealegacy.org*.

Careful attention to language focusing on continuing organizational values, enhancing future opportunities, or relief of suffering will appeal to most gift planning prospects. Appeals should show the immediate impact and long-term outcomes from gifts and what successful achievement of the mission will deliver.

The content of gift planning ads can cover a broad range of areas. However, ads seem to be most effective when they put a face on mission and integrate it with helping the donor achieve a personal planning objective. Just remember to keep your ads focused on prospect motivations using language that is most likely to appeal to the audience of your publication or piece.

Reply Cards and Envelopes

Whatever medium you use to market gift planning opportunities, there should be a response mechanism using that medium. So if it is a print piece, offer a printed confidential reply card. If it is web- or email-based, provide an electronic reply mechanism with a dedicated landing page.

Gift planning prospects usually want to be private. Whatever means they use to respond should be designed in such a way that their personal information is not revealed. The response tool should also be targeted. For example, if the ad is about increasing retirement income while supporting the cause, then the check boxes on the reply card should include only what is needed to get more information about increasing retirement income. By keeping the reply mechanism on point with the ad, it will produce a higher response rate.

Website

A website is your online brochure. Most of your marketing will drive prospects to your website for more information. Even if you have a gift planning presence in social media, you need a basic gift planning website that is linked to all of your other social media and the remaining sections of your organization's website.

Due to the constantly changing laws and regulations surrounding charitable gift planning, we strongly recommend that you purchase a gift planning website from one of the many vendors in the marketplace. Brian has done extensive work with Virtual Giving and Brian and Robert have presented on behalf of Crescendo Interactive, two of the premier web vendors in the space. There are also excellent offerings from the Stelter Company, Pentera, EDS, PG Calc, and others. The vendors can create sites that look and feel like your site. The key is to find a vendor that fits well with your nonprofit and your constituency.

When evaluating these vendors, consider the materials provided and your audience. For example, Virtual Giving tends to use a "keep it simple" approach with less technical information. Crescendo, on the other hand, tends to include a tremendous amount of detailed information on its websites. What does that mean for you? If you have a population that wants to delve into every last detail of gift planning (for example, an engineering college), then you might look at Crescendo. If you have an audience that is less worried about the tax implications of a grantor-retained charitable lead trust (for example, an art museum), then you might look at Virtual Giving.

If you just are not comfortable purchasing a site and want to create your own, consider Planned Giving in a Box. It is a step-by-step program to help your nonprofit build a gift planning program in an hour a week for fifty-two weeks. Filled with template documents, including sample website language, it might be the answer if you do not want to create everything from scratch but also do not want to hire a vendor to provide your site.

Social Media and Networking Sites

The use of social media has exploded in the last few years. Just ten to fifteen years ago, charities were debating whether gift planning web pages made

---

Use Real Donor Photos and Stories

I have been a Crescendo user for many years and have also used other vendors to provide website content to appeal to my donors and prospects. To maximize its effectiveness, I use as many real donor photos and stories as I can. This more closely ties the content to my nonprofit and its mission. Stock photography and sample donor stories are good filler if you do not have stories of your own, but the savvy audience wants to hear real stories about gifts to your nonprofit.

—Robert

 stories from the real world

sense—and now every nonprofit with a gift planning program has one. In a few more years, there will be no debate that charities need to be active in social networking. Now is the time to create or enhance your social networking presence. It will help increase your reach to all generational cohorts, particularly Millennials and Gen Xers, the next generations of givers and leaders in the charitable sector. It will also help you with the Leading and Trailing Boomers, who have some of the largest Facebook usage increases of any cohorts. Many nonprofits have found great success adding gift planning messaging to their existing social media presence. LinkedIn has proven to be particularly useful to mine prospect information and reconnect with lost prospects in a nonthreatening manner. Social media gives your nonprofit the opportunity to share outcomes-based stories with potential planned gift donors in an easy, appealing, inexpensive way.

Multimedia

With the advent of Facebook, YouTube, Pinterest, and other multimedia sites, along with the proliferation of streaming and cloud computing, it is more important than ever for gift planning programs to include multimedia in their marketing and advertising. There is nothing more powerful than an outcomes-based video clip showing how a past gift has changed the world.

> ### Engage Millennials and Gen Xers
>
> If you wait too long to market to your prospects, by the time you start to reach out to them they will already be set with their favorite charities. It is not too soon to be marketing and engaging Millennials and Gen X donors.
>
>

With the technology available today, it is possible for every nonprofit to produce inexpensive videos to show the impact and outcomes of gifts. These stories will motivate your prospects to become donors and add great value to the gift planning effort.

Mass Email

At one time, there was a robust market for mass emails in gift planning. It allowed you to reach a broad audience and determine interest. However, with the increased sophistication of email SPAM filtering, along with federal regulation, it no longer makes a great deal of sense. Using targeted email to a select audience will be far more effective, as discussed in **Chapter Fifteen**.

Marketing Grid

When marketing on a moves management platform, it is important to have a plan and track your results. To do so, each piece needs to serve a designated step in the moves management process. When a marketing piece tries to do too many things or take too many steps at once, it loses focus and effectiveness.

Each piece in the gift planning marketing effort should have clear content, an identified audience, a logical schedule, a reasonable budget, and identified measures of success. While tracking success sounds straightforward, in this era of multichannel marketing, it is very difficult. Most fundraising software is designed to track each marketing piece individually, and the only outcome it can record is a gift. You will need to work with your database provider or build systems that allow you to track the different multichannel touches for each prospect to evaluate results. It is no longer possible to measure success by the number of responses to a single piece. Instead, you need to look at the entire marketing plan, all of the touches from the various communications tools and vehicles, and evaluate over the long term whether the overall effect is moving the suspect to a prospect, prospect to donor, and donor to repeat donor.

If the donor-focused gift planning marketing effort is properly designed, you will be able to clearly measure performance from an increased number of:

◆ gift planning inquiries

◆ gift planning asks and commitments

◆ complex asset gifts and commitments

◆ strategy and planning discussions

Without an effective plan, you will continue to produce random acts of marketing that can be tracked individually but do not help move the entire effort forward over time. Each piece has its own response rate, but the overall success requires evaluation over the entire moves management spectrum.

To assist you in building your plan, Chapter Eight of the *Resource Book* offers a template gift planning marketing grid.

To Recap

◆ Gift planning marketing starts at the top of the gift planning pyramid, but if you do not market to all levels, your program will not be sustainable.

◆ Avoid marketing gift planning tools and vehicles and instead market to help individuals integrate their philanthropy into their overall tax, estate, and financial planning or to meet personal planning objectives.

◆ By integrating gift planning marketing into existing marketing and outreach pieces, you can reach the broadest audience of potential prospects at the lowest cost.

◆ Every marketing piece should have a reply mechanism using the same medium.

◆ Websites, social media presence, and multimedia approaches are well established and vital to the success of a multichannel, donor-focused gift planning marketing effort.

◆ Video can be one of the most powerful marketing tools, showing the long-term outcomes created by gifts.

◆ Your program should have a marketing grid and measures of success for its gift planning outreach plan.

Chapter Fifteen

Marketing to Identified Prospects Without Major Capacity

In This Chapter

- → Segment your loyals

- → Target your outreach to identified segments

- → Marketing tools for loyals

- → Appropriate use of social media

Once you establish your marketing for "everyone else," the next tier in the pyramid deals with loyals who do not have the capacity to make major gifts. This group typically makes up the vast majority of your gift planning prospects. For most nonprofits, approximately 90 percent of loyals are not identified in a typical wealth screening (capacity of $100,000 over five years/ $20,000 per year).

Because there are so many loyals, it would be impossible for you to meet with each of them personally and discuss gift planning. Most nonprofits prioritize visits with loyals who also have higher capacity, as discussed in the next chapter. To target the remaining loyals, you will use gift planning marketing to reach this important group.

There are many tools to reach your loyals. You want to select tools and messages that work most effectively for your selected audience. If your audience is large enough, you can also test different approaches and tools to see what garners the best results. This chapter will explore some of the more common options. Once you establish what you want to send to your loyals, place those pieces on your moves management gift planning marketing grid.

Postcards

Over the last several years, postcards with reply devices have become the solicitation method of choice for gift planning programs. Because the prospect does not have to open the postcard to get the message, they are more likely to be read.

> ### Go Granular!
>
> We work with several universities, all of which have multiple colleges and units that constitute the school. When we have instituted postcard mailers, some have tried to take a shortcut and use one postcard for the entire university, and response rates have been very low. When we instead create a postcard focusing on the identity and mission of each college or unit, response rates increase dramatically, highlighting the importance of mission when crafting postcards.
>
> The same result has been true when working with multiple-hospital health care systems. Those that market using the identities of the individual hospitals do far better than those marketing the system.
>
> Gift planning donors are making an investment in the long-term future of your organization. They want to be sure that their gifts, even if for general purposes, are still benefiting the part of your nonprofit that is important to them.
>
>  stories from the real world

Effective postcards illustrate an outcome from a prior gift to your organization while helping a prospect meet a personal planning objective. They use powerful, professional photography and end with a clear call to action. Because it is a gift planning postcard, it should have a confidential reply mechanism, including a way to visit your website.

Select your postcard messages from those outlined in **Chapter Fourteen**. Mail the postcard only to the audience targeted by the postcard's message. For example, if the postcard is about increasing retirement income today, use a postcard design and target list for the Traditionalists in your prospect pool. If the postcard is about increasing future retirement income, then the message should be much more outcomes-based and targeted at Older and Younger Boomers in the loyals group.

Email Follow-Up

While postcards are a great tool, it is important to follow them up with an email. As a general rule, send your follow-up email between two and three weeks following the mailing of the postcard. This time frame is long enough so that those who would reply to the actual postcard will have done so but not so long that readers will have forgotten receiving the postcard.

The email should reaffirm the message of the postcard and provide a hot link to your gift planning website. The more personalized the messaging, the greater the likelihood the message will be read.

Brochures and Fulfillment Pieces

Even with the explosion of electronic media, prospects in all generational cohorts still prefer to get gift planning materials in print. While this is rapidly evolving, it is still your best practice for right now.

Even if you offer e-brochures on the website you purchase from a vendor, you still need a group of materials that you can share with prospects about gift planning. Some of these materials are "leave-behind" pieces that your team includes in a standard development visit package. Others are for responding to prospects who ask for more information about gift planning. For most nonprofits right now, these pieces should be designed with the Leading Boomers in mind, since they are at their peak earning and giving years.

General Brochure

The first piece you should develop is a general gift planning brochure. It is the first introduction to gift planning and "leave behind" piece described above. The brochure should include information about your mission, how planned gifts have helped your organization achieve that mission, and real-life

We Tested Mailings with List Splitting

Meridian Health is now an eight-hospital health system, having recently acquired two hospitals. One of the formerly independent hospitals had done very well in marketing to loyals without major capacity and encouraging planned gifts, so there was already a strong awareness among the group about the case for support for the hospital. To test a postcard, it was mailed to two groups of loyals—one for this hospital with a strong group of loyals, and the other to a hospital that as of yet had not established its case for support. While the mailing was equal to both segments, the hospital with an established case and loyals produced a return that was nearly five times greater. Not only were the responses positive, but several new gift annuities and many new bequest expectancies were established.

—Robert

stories from
the real world

outcomes created by planned gifts. You are trying to "hook" prospects so that they will ask for more information and you can start to build a relationship.

Try to avoid including technical information in your general brochure. Most of your prospects, if they desire that information at all, will want to get it from their own advisors. Include just two or three lines on each of the personal planning objectives and then name the tools that help the prospect achieve that goal while also being charitable.

Fulfillment Pieces

Once a prospect requests more information, you need to follow up with a phone call and have an additional piece to send. These are your fulfillment pieces. We prefer to have a fulfillment package ready before a mailing ever goes out.

For example, if you send out a mailing about increasing future retirement income to Leading Boomers, you would have a cover letter and descriptive piece ready to send to those who ask for more information. The descriptive piece is often a "one-pager" that describes how a particular gift planning tool meets the prospect's personal planning objective. In this case, it might discuss both a flexible charitable gift annuity and a flip charitable remainder unitrust. But the one-pager would do so in a simple format without technical language.

You then follow up the fulfillment piece with a phone call and request a visit to explain the materials. If the prospect is local, you may skip sending the fulfillment piece all together and bring it with you to the next visit. Once you have the piece, you will end up using it in several ways.

Phone-calling Programs

It is only in the last several years that phone calling for gift planning has emerged as a marketing tool. Until recently, gift planning was considered too specialized and personal to allow for general phone calling. It also is not necessarily something that can be completed in a single phone call, so most nonprofits and firms were hesitant to embrace it.

However, with direct mail continuing to decline in effectiveness, several phone-calling firms have made a conscious effort to enter the gift planning calling field and are getting results. Most phone-calling programs now report a 15 percent or higher response rate from loyal prospects, which opens the door for further conversations.

Measurable Increase in Response Rate

When using the follow-up email three weeks after the postcard in the Meridian Health example, there was a measurable increase in the response rate.

stories from
the real world

A Guide to Planning Your Will or Estate

Over the years, the best piece to offer as a fulfillment premium in a direct mail campaign or leave-behind has been *A Guide to Planning Your Will or Estate*. Several vendors offer excellent samples to modify for your use, or you can also work with a trust and estate attorney to craft your own. Since everyone should have a will, it is a piece that should appeal to all.

important

Your phone program should be unique to your nonprofit. The most effective models use a preliminary letter to introduce the idea of the call, an initial call with multiple tries if necessary, fulfillment materials after the call, and a follow-up either by staff of the nonprofit or by consulting staff trained in gift planning to build a relationship and close the gift. Some nonprofits have used their own staff or alumni instead of a telemarketing firm with good results. The key is to remember that it is not a sale but an opportunity for prospects to build on the legacy created by their loyal annual support.

Texts and Tweets

While texts and tweets are being used for direct fundraising, it does not appear that they are effective tools for gift planning at this time. Many prospects react negatively to an unsolicited text, particularly one that asks them to consider a charitable gift. They are more open to sending a text to complete a gift.

Tweeting about philanthropy has become more common, but because gift planning is for a targeted audience of loyals, there has not been great success generating leads using Twitter. Even so, ignore social media at your peril. As we discussed in **Chapter Fourteen**, it is a quickly evolving technology, and experimenting with different messages to select audiences across multiple platforms may prove fruitful if your nonprofit has the right message and audience.

To Recap

◆ Segment your loyals and target your outreach to the identified segments.

◆ Postcards are an effective tool to reach loyals and can be customized for different segments.

◆ Brochures are still useful, particularly for a gift planning audience.

◆ Put your fulfillment packages in place before sending your gift planning mailings.

◆ Properly executed phone-calling programs can yield a large number of responses and active leads from your loyals group.

◆ Social media is an evolving and important tool for your gift planning audience. Stay abreast of current developments and use it as appropriate.

Chapter Sixteen

Marketing to Major and Principal Prospects

This Chapter

- ◆ Why mass marketing doesn't work for loyal major and principal prospects
- ◆ Personalized marketing
- ◆ Working in a donor-focused way
- ◆ Avoid overmarketing

Loyal major and principal gift prospects are the most important people to your charitable gift planning effort. They have the capacity and the inclination to make institution-changing gifts during their lifetime and at death. You need to treat them differently than you do "everyone else" and your other "loyals." You need to market to them one-on-one and in-person (which really isn't marketing at all, is it?).

Why Mass Marketing Doesn't Work for Loyal Major and Principal Prospects

Your loyal major and principal prospects already believe in the mission of your organization. They have attended your events, read your case for support, seen the results of your good works, and invested in the cause. Sending them postcards, newsletters, tweets, Facebook posts, emails, and other generic materials about giving to your organization is not likely to prompt a thoughtful, targeted gift to the area of your mission that is important to the donor and moves the relationship forward. Instead, it will prompt a "go away" gift, making it harder to engage the donor in the next level of conversation about a true investment and potentially a planned gift.

Personalized Marketing

No two donors are alike. So our approach should not be general and the same for all. Did you know that no two lions have the same pattern of whiskers? The muzzle of a lion is like a fingerprint. Even the king of the jungle is unique, and certainly we would all be careful if we were to approach one.

Legacy Gifts

I attended a presentation by a high-net-worth philanthropist at the peak of the last recession. She was talking about the impact of the recession on philanthropy. She commented that several nonprofits she regularly supported had reached out and let her know that if she was negatively impacted by the recession, she could alter her pledge payment schedule or reduce her giving—so she did. At the same time, another nonprofit approached her and suggested that because times were tough, it needed her to increase her support more than ever—so she did.

Someone in the audience then asked her if she had adjusted her legacy gifts. She said yes, but not in the way that you would think. She shared that legacies are not "left" at death but are "built" over the course of one's lifetime. When times are tough, and nonprofits need support the most, that is when a true philanthropist steps up and makes a new, additional commitment to ensure the good works of the nonprofit continue. That is the most meaningful legacy a philanthropist can create. An important reminder: you get what you ask for, and you ask your prospects to build their legacy over their lifetimes and complete it with a capstone gift at their passing.

—Brian

 stories from the real world

If you feel compelled to send gift planning-specific marketing to your major and principal prospects, make sure that it is both personalized and targeted. With the advent of digital printing and electronic media, you can easily and readily send marketing materials that are customized to the prospect in question.

Do We Know Our Donors?

We may think that we know our donors, but what we see isn't always the case. And we often follow commonly believed misperceptions that we need to be careful to avoid. For example, most think of zebras as animals that look like white horses with black stripes, but actually zebras are all black with white stripes—they even have black skin under their white hair. So, who are your donors? We need to be donor-focused in our approach and pay attention to their similarities and their differences. We have even learned that we need to be sensitive to our approach as it relates to gender.

As always, materials should be talking about your mission. But beyond that, they should include prospect names and be directly related to a personal planning objective that is important to the prospect. For example, you would likely not send a piece about increasing retirement income. However, you might send information about how donors can fulfill their charitable legacies while also maximizing their children's inheritances.

Keep it Personal

I have often used two methods that have proven to be effective in impacting the donors I have cultivated. First, if using materials about your organization's mission, take the time to handwrite a personal note and attach it to the piece so the donor knows that you personally hand-selected and sent the information. Second, whenever possible, send individual letters that include an article or other item that you know is of interest to your donor. With all the junk mail we receive, it will stand out; and if you know your donors, they will truly appreciate your thinking about them.

—Robert

 practical tip

Avoid Overmarketing

Your nonprofit's multichannel marketing effort should already be delivering a lot of information to your major and principal prospects about the impact and outcomes your nonprofit is delivering. It is important not to overwhelm them with information from the fundraising side of the shop as well. When you send reams of information to busy and highly successful people, even personalized marketing, they tune it all out and stop reading anything you send—from the fundraising side or from the general marketing side.

Most of your fundraising with these individuals is being done one on one. By allowing your multichannel process to keep you front of mind with your best prospects and introducing gift planning opportunities at the appropriate times in personal conversations, you'll maximize the opportunity for the message to be heard above the din of the regular marketing effort. Doing too much could cause the entire message to be lost.

To Recap

◆ Do not use mass marketing of gift planning with your high-net-worth prospects.

◆ If you insist on marketing to this group, it should be customized with their names and with an appropriate message.

◆ Use one-on-one conversations to suggest when gift planning might be appropriate to meet donors' personal planning and charitable goals.

Is Your Organization the Choice of the New Generation?

When I think of overmarketing, sodas like Pepsi come to mind. Over the years, millions of dollars have been spent to encourage the beverage-buying public to choose Pepsi over its competition. It has been marketed as the choice of the new generation. More recently soda, with all of its sugar, has come under scrutiny from a health-and-nutrition-conscious public. Originally developed by a young pharmacist named Caleb Bradham, it was called Brad's Drink and was a beverage to aid digestion and boost energy. Because of the pepsin and kola nut ingredients in the concoction, it was renamed Pepsi-Cola. Its recipe is now far removed from the original, with several versions and many flavors to tempt buyers. Most sodas were invented by pharmacists as a means to help people. So how did we get to a place where we now have concerns of overdevelopment and overmarketing? If we remember that we want to educate our donors to encourage their interest, and if we remain donor-focused, we stand a better chance of staying on target with the pace and quantity of the messages that we deliver.

–Robert

observation

Part Five

Helpful Tips from the Field

To this point, we have presented the elements required to start a gift planning program for your nonprofit. The last two chapters will focus on providing tips for your particular sector so you can easily build your program over the next year.

Chapter Seventeen

Sector-specific Gift Planning Tips

In This Chapter

- ---→ Understanding gift planning in your sector
- ---→ Blending with a relational model in fundraising
- ---→ Blending with a transactional model in fundraising
- ---→ Blending with a membership model in fundraising

Each sector within the nonprofit world has its own unique approach to fundraising and gift planning. In fact, there are so many sectors and subsectors, we almost elected not to cover the material at all. But knowing that some general comments about the key sectors would help you in your work, we identified the largest sectors and share our thoughts.

The six largest sectors in fundraising include higher education, health care, social/human services, the arts/sciences/museums, religion, and community foundations. Each sector has built a fundraising model that works for donors who typically support nonprofits in that sector. The most common models are the transactional model, the relational model, and the membership model.

The transactional model was once the most common type of fundraising. The nonprofit organization presented a need and the prospect either made a gift to support it or did not. Sometimes the need was the general mission and in other cases it was for a particular project or effort. As we noted in **Chapter Nine,** with the emergence of the New Philanthropist generations, the transactional model is now in decline.

While donors are motivated more than ever by impact and outcomes, meaning that tangible results are required in order to secure gifts, they also want and need those gifts to be integrated into their tax, estate, and financial planning to ensure that their charitable giving is part of their larger strategy. Nonprofits that ignore this shift will find it more and more difficult to raise the transformative gifts they desire in the coming years. The transactional model is the least effective in building donor trust, the core element required by the New Philanthropists.

The relational model focuses on building meaningful relationships between the nonprofit organization and the prospect. Over time, that relationship breeds trust, which allows the nonprofit to ask the prospect to make more significant investments in the organization and its priorities. And because the parties know each other well, those investments can be synchronized with the prospect's planning to ensure that personal planning goals for the prospect and family are met. Without this trust, built over time, it will become much more difficult to raise large gifts, which is why you see so many charities moving to this model.

The membership model focuses on providing modest benefits to regular supporters by making them members of either a giving group (such as a giving club) or the entity itself (such as a museum or theater). The goal is to effectively steward these regular supporters as members so that over time they are willing to become larger and more meaningful donors. Higher-level members receive additional benefits, but rarely are the benefits more valuable than the increased support. The membership model helps the organization build trust as members recognize the good work that the organization is doing, eventually building a deeper relationship between the organization and the member, which can lead to transformational gifts.

Higher Education

The higher education sector tends to use a relational model of fundraising. An administrator, fundraiser, or volunteer forges a relationship with a prospect that is cultivated using a moves management approach, eventually leading to a series of growing investments in the school. This forms a bond between the donor and the institution, a relationship upon which everything else is built.

For gift planning purposes, this relationship is vital to your success, as it allows the school to help donors integrate their philanthropy into their overall tax, estate, and financial planning in a way that does not happen in a transactional model.

For this relationship model to work best, time is needed to reach out to donors in a way that appeals to their sense of involvement with the college or university. The advantage of knowing the age of most of the alumni can also allow for segmenting in your approach that will help you work with a graduating class where several classmates are involved as volunteers in your outreach to their peers.

Health Care

The health care sector tends to use a transactional model of fundraising. In today's society, people pick up and move their families on a regular basis, which makes relational fundraising difficult for hospitals and other health-related entities. If a prospect won't be using your facility in five years, the opportunities for legacy gifts tend to be less than they would be in higher education, which benefits from lifelong relationships with alumni. Add to that specialized medicine, so even if a hospital does have a long-term patient, that person still may go elsewhere for noncritical care, and it is apparent why so many health care-related charities focus on a transactional model. For nonprofits in more rural areas with stable populations, it is possible to use a relational and a transactional approach, depending on the donor.

From a gift planning perspective, it is difficult to encourage long-term investments from prospects that may not live in the service area for an extended period. Instead of beneficiary designations on wills and retirement plans, you may instead focus on life-income gifts and life insurance policies. You are less likely to try to find integrated solutions since plans will likely change after a prospect moves out of the area and you lose touch.

If you are fortunate enough to determine that you have many loyal annual donors who have given over several years and continue to value the mission of your hospital or health care organization, stories about grateful patients can remind these constituents of why they have been giving and why their gifts are making a difference in their own care and the care of their families and friends. In addition, many retirees enjoy volunteering at health care facilities and are good prospects for building relationships that allow for gift planning in the traditional sense.

Social/Human Services

In our experience, most social and human service agencies do not proactively pursue gift planning. You get the majority of your reimbursement and support from insurance companies and government agencies, relying on very modest support from individual gifts. In such cases, you do not have a robust group of loyal donors to create an audience for gift planning. To move into the gift planning space, start by building an active annual giving program and creating institutional priorities that can be funded from individual gifts. With the changing reimbursement laws and state budget challenges, it may be an opportune time to add gift planning as a revenue stream.

> ### Passionate Volunteers
>
> We have seen quite a number of retirees get involved as auxilians to support our hospitals across Meridian Health. These volunteers exhibit a passion to support our cause that is second to none. In fact, four of our auxiliaries at Southern Ocean Medical Center recently pledged to raise $2.5 million as the lead gift for a new cancer center. For many this was the only way they might be able to make a gift, but for some this was an eye opener for how they could also make a personal gift that would help them in their situation as well as their favorite hospital.
>
> —Robert
>
>  stories from the real world

The Arts/Sciences/Museums

This sector tends to focus on a membership model of fundraising. This model encourages prospects to become members in exchange for a suite of benefits, such as better seating or access. These benefits can make moving these individuals into donors difficult. First, they are used to getting something in exchange for their membership, which means they often are not philanthropically minded. Second, they feel that they have already made contributions with their memberships.

When identifying prospects for gift planning from your membership list, you need to look at the benefits you offer. If you have individuals who are members and do not use the benefits, they are good gift planning prospects. Similarly, if you have a membership level where the benefits are not sufficient to warrant the cost of membership, those individuals are also likely philanthropic and good targets for gift planning conversations.

Creating a legacy society or heritage club can also help you advance donors who are comfortable in a membership model. The exclusivity of special showings or viewings can increase interest, and benefits can be related to providing for others to enjoy what they have enjoyed during their time. Other benefits that are visible for regular members to see and hear about will also help increase awareness of gift planning and its value to the organization.

Religion

Historically, individuals give more to religious organizations than to any other sector. Be it through tithing a percentage of income each year or passing the offering plate each week, religious organizations do a wonderful job of garnering regular annual support.

Ironically, despite this cadre of regular givers, most religious organizations are not particularly successful in charitable gift planning. Why? Because they do not ask, and they do not do a good job showing the impact gifts have or the long-term outcomes they create. The giving comes from a sense of obligation rather than from a culture of philanthropy. They also don't employ many professional fundraisers to assist in relationship building and a process of donor cultivation.

With the best gift planning prospects coming from loyal regular donors, most members of religious organizations should be the focus of activities to cultivate planned gifts. As the expression goes, these organizations are in "high cotton," meaning they are ready for the pickin'. In their 1994 book *The Seven Faces of Philanthropy*, Prince and File present "The Devout," who give due to their religious beliefs and out of a sense of moral obligation. And while many people are raised making an offering as the plate is passed to continue the ministry of the church or pledging an annual amount to support the synagogue, only when there is care taken to craft a message to remind donors why their gifts are needed and how they will be used will the soil be fertile to yield the results that it should. But without a doubt, this tremendously loyal audience with a strong belief in the mission should be actively pursued for planned gifts.

Community Foundations

Community foundations tend to have the most donor-focused, philanthropic planning approach of all the sectors. They forge relationships with their donors and their advisors and assist individuals in creating a philanthropic legacy for all of the charitable causes they believe in that are in their communities. Part of this stems from the historical fact that many community foundations do not have fundraising priorities of their own to compete with the missions of local charities. But there is also a culture of philanthropy at community foundations that is not always present at other nonprofits because their primary role is to promote philanthropy, not provide a particular service.

If you work for a community foundation and do not have a robust philanthropic planning program, it should be your number-one priority. The greatest impediment we have seen to these programs is the idea in some quarters that community foundations "attract wealth" rather than fundraise. This approach has caused some community foundations to have limited annual giving programs and limited pools of loyal donors to draw upon. You need to build up your annual giving program quickly or look to see who the loyal donors are to other charities in your community and approach them with a philanthropic planning approach.

To Recap

◆ Each fundraising sector has unique challenges in building gift planning programs.

◆ These challenges can be identified and overcome with planning.

◆ Depending upon your sector, a relational or transactional model, or both, may be appropriate.

◆ Do not use your fundraising sector as an excuse not to pursue gift planning.

Epilogue

The Time Is Now

In This Chapter

- ···➔ The three legs of the gift planning stool

- ···➔ Helpful tips

- ···➔ Where do I go for additional resources?

- ···➔ Your opportunity...the time is now!

We began our discovery of charitable gift planning by reflecting on the thoughts you might have as you take your first step on a hike. How you may start on the trail without much in mind other than getting to the end or the goal, but how, upon reflection, the sights and sounds with every step along the way can help shape you as a person and sharpen your experience. If you look at a map before you head out, there is a better opportunity to see more of what the trail has to offer. We hope that *Getting Started in Charitable Gift Planning* is your map on your journey so that you might not only learn along your gift planning trail but that you might also enhance your skill sets and spirit to work with donors.

From page one, we have consistently reminded you that charitable gift planning must be focused on your mission, not the tools or gift vehicles—so much so that we left descriptions of the tools and vehicles to the accompanying *Resource Book*. Once a prospect buys into the mission, you can apply the tools from the *Resource Book* to assist the prospect in meeting personal planning goals.

To be successful, you must have a cause that will benefit from long-term support, a strategic plan with visionary goals, and leadership that is engaged and believes in building an endowment. With these elements, you can pursue a charitable gift planning program. If you do not have these elements, start by working with your board to create them. They are the prerequisites for success.

We divided *Getting Started in Charitable Gift Planning* into five parts to help you organize your thoughts and establish a baseline of understanding the concept. In **Part One**, Getting Started in Gift Planning, we defined gift planning, established why it is important to your prospects, and described its role within the overall fundraising program in your organization. We offered a readiness questionnaire to help you to

> ### It's About Long-term Support
>
> Charitable gift planning is about long-term support of your mission.
>
>

determine if your organization was ready to launch a successful program.

The first step in your journey is to write your internal case for support. It will keep you and the organization focused on gift planning through leadership changes and tough economic times, when it would be easy to give up on gift planning. It will also serve your successor well. Even though you may not be planning to leave your nonprofit, the reality is that the average tenure of a fundraiser is sixteen months. You need to create a documented trail for your successor to follow. Anything less would be unfair to the organization and its donors.

Infrastructure

In **Part Two**, Infrastructure, we presented how building the infrastructure and creating a culture of donor-focused gift planning is vital to your success.

We reminded you why ethics and integrity are hallmarks of establishing trust in your relationships with donors and how your donor service and skill in collaboration are more important than being the most knowledgeable technical expert. If you are not a gift planning expert, do not pretend to be one. Instead, look for opportunities to learn and grow with your program. Remember that 80 percent of all planned gifts are basic beneficiary designations

> ### Don't Try to Skip to the End
>
> Without proper infrastructure, your gift planning program will fail.
>
>

in wills, living trusts, retirement plans, life insurance policies, donor-advised funds, payable-on-death accounts, and transfer-on-death assets. You understand these types of gifts and can guide your prospects through them. When you have tougher questions, first try to find the answers yourself. Then, after you have done your homework, confirm with an expert that you found the right solution. This will help you grow as a gift planner and gain confidence. Be sure to understand and follow the rules of ethics as you learn these more complex concepts.

With your role articulated, define roles for your board, volunteer leadership, and professional advisors in your gift planning program. You need well-placed champions for your program to be successful. The best champions have set up their planned gifts for your nonprofit. You now know the types of professional

> ### Be a Philanthropist!
>
> It is much easier to ask others for planned gifts when you have completed one yourself.
>
>

advisors and their roles in the planning process, when to call them, and how you can support them in their work while they support your organization. We explained the roles of the CEO, CDO, director of development, development officer, board member, and volunteer.

There are several key documents that are absolutely vital to the success of your gift planning effort, including a gift counting and valuation policy, a gift acceptance policy, gift agreements, and an estate administration process. Samples for all of these documents are in Chapter Six of the *Resource Book* and should be set up before you work with prospects.

Infrastructure is not complete until you have measures of success. This means setting up your tracking reports for activity, visits, proposals, asks, completed gifts, and stewardship. People respond to performance metrics. Be sure to have them and track them.

Working with Prospects

Part Three, Prospect Interaction, explained the characteristics of the New Philanthropist and why generational differences need to be accounted for if we are to succeed in the twenty-first century.

> ### Start with Your Organization's Loyals
>
> Always select your gift planning prospect audience based on loyalty *before* you start to segment the list for generational cohorts, gender, no children, etc. Loyals are the best prospects for planned gifts.
>
>

Identifying gift planning prospects starts with your existing gift planning donors. In a mature gift planning program, 50 percent of all new commitments come from existing gift planning donors. From there, consider the loyal donors to your annual fund. Gift planning prospects have one thing in common–a very strong affinity to your mission and dedication to it for the long term.

With your loyals identified, coded, and segmented in your database, send them the most targeted messages you can afford. The very best gift planning prospects, the ones with the highest loyalty and a high capacity, should be the first ones you visit, and then be sure to visit them often. Gift planning results do not come from sitting behind your desk sending out marketing pieces or updating your website; they come from personal conversations with loyal prospects you ask to make long-term investments in the cause.

> ### Be a Stranger to Your Own Desk!
>
> You know you're a successful gift planner when your colleagues are surprised to see you behind your desk and not out visiting with prospects.
>
> **observation**

Setting up gift planning visits is a marathon and should be your highest priority. You need to have a system in place to ensure that you are calling for visits every day and setting yourself up for future success.

As you will not be able to visit every prospect, cross-train your other staff, board members, local professional advisors, and volunteers on the signs that your prospect might be interested in gift planning. They will be a wonderful referral source for you. Before you know it, you'll have many planned gifts coming in the door.

The final step in your gift planning process is to create a means to steward those donors who have included your organization in their plans or set up endowments for your organization's benefit. Since most planned gifts are revocable, you will lose donors over time unless you have an effective stewardship program. Nonprofits that ignore stewardship do so at their own peril, particularly

> ### When It All Comes Together for the Donor
>
> Most planned gifts happen when a donor believes in the mission, is loyal to the cause, needs to meet a personal planning objective, and has a life event close to the time when the fundraiser calls for a visit.
>
>

when the gifts are coming from New Philanthropists (those born 1946–present). Concierge stewardship and our seven touches philosophy will keep your mission in front of your donors and remind them how valuable they are to your organization.

Donor-focused Marketing

Part Four, Marketing Gift Planning, presented the four tiers of the gift planning marketing pyramid and how you should have three distinct approaches: marketing to everyone, marketing to identified prospects without major capacity, and marketing to major and principal prospects.

> ### Marketing Is *Not* Gift Planning
>
> Effective gift planning marketing is a process whereby you proactively share gift planning information with likely gift planning prospects, and if they respond, you then reach out to them individually. People make gifts because they are asked, not because they get a great postcard in the mail.
>
>

While ideally you would be able to visit all of your identified loyal prospects, the reality is that you probably do not have enough time or staff resources to do so. For those you cannot reach personally, you need to invest in a robust, multichannel marketing and communications plan to get the word out.

Your promotional materials need to include an assortment of electronic and print materials based on your organization's moves management platform. This will help move prospects along by educating them about the opportunities and cultivating their interest sufficiently for them to reach out to you to ask for more information and one-on-one support. You need to have a systematic and consistent communications plan.

Helpful Tips

In **Part Five**, Helpful Tips from the Field, we shared gift planning tips from our more than forty years of experience and the nuances of gift planning in higher education, health care, social/human services, the arts, religion, and community foundations.

Once you have reached this point, you have developed a *stage one* gift planning program for your nonprofit. To be sustainable, we suggested you develop a multiyear plan for your gift planning efforts, covering each of the three legs of the gift planning stool. This will allow your program to grow in sophistication and success each and every year.

> ### Seven Touches
>
> If your gift planning outreach is not multichannel and does not include at least seven touches, your prospects will never realize you are communicating with them. These are "random acts of marketing." Is saving money by completing fewer than seven touches really cost effective if your prospects never get the message?
>
>

Where Do I Go for Additional Resources?

Throughout this book, we have offered resources to delve deeper into the topics. As you continue to grow in your knowledge and determine that you have built a donor-focused development program that has a strong infrastructure to support your organization and the top tier of your donor base, then *The Philanthropic Planning Companion* can be an excellent reference. Until you have reached that point, we suggest that you use the *Resource Book*. Written in concert with this book, the *Resource Book* provides lists, documents, charts, and templates to guide you in your journey.

Your Opportunity...The Time is *Now*

With the knowledge and the tools, it is time to get to work. Books are helpful, and conferences and speakers can be motivating, but nothing takes the place of rolling up your sleeves and building your program.

Take what you have before you and apply it to your development practice.

> *Opportunity is missed by most people because it is dressed in overalls and looks like work.*
>
> —Thomas Edison, American inventor credited with 1,093 patents

The Schervish and Havens study estimates that at least $6 trillion will be directed to charities from generous donors who understand the importance of giving to make their communities and their world a better place. Many of these donors, when educated about a gift planning approach, will welcome the opportunity to meet their own needs while also making a difference. Every organization can benefit from this enormous transfer of wealth through a gift planning program. The amount that loyal friends designate for your goals depends on you. These gifts will add to your endowment, produce increased annual support, and engage donors for the long term. Even more importantly, they will provide stable revenue during times of economic downturn.

Annual giving provides immediate satisfaction and operational support. Major giving takes time to develop, but it provides for special projects and capital growth. Gift planning and planned gifts offer the richest rewards if you follow a plan and a donor-focused approach. The process and steps we have laid out, if followed, will lead your nonprofit to gift planning results.

We wish you much success as you build your program. It is up to you.

Index

If you enjoyed this book, you'll want to pick up *Getting Started in Charitable Gift Planning: The Resource Book,* published by CharityChannel Press as part of the popular **In the Trenches**™ series for nonprofit-sector practitioners.

Getting Started in Charitable Gift Planning

The Resource Book

Brian M. Sagrestano, JD, CFRE

Robert E. Wahlers, MS, CFRE

Supplemental resources that assist you by:
- Explaining the basic tools of charitable gift planning
- Answering common gift planning questions
- Providing tools to build your gift planning program
- Defining key terms important in gift planning conversations

And so much more!

CharityChannel.com/bookstore

CharityChannel PRESS™

You also might be interested in our just-released *CharityChannel's Quick Guide to Developing Your Case for Support,* by Margaret Guellich and Linda Lysakowski.

CharityChannel's

Quick Guide to

Developing Your Case for Support

Margaret Guellich, CFRE
Linda Lysakowski, ACFRE

- Learn what a case for support is, and isn't
- Determine who should write your case for support
- Prepare to gather all the information you need to write your case
- Build a case that tells your story to your various "publics"

CharityChannel.com/bookstore

CharityChannel
P R E S S

Did you know that CharityChannel Press is the fastest growing publisher of books for busy nonprofit professionals? Here are some of our most popular titles.

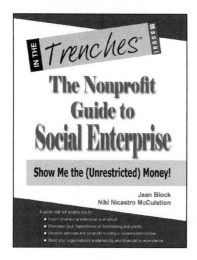
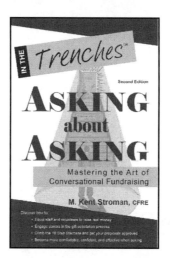
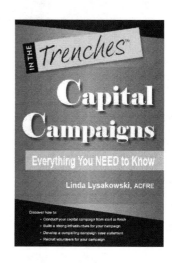

CharityChannel.com/bookstore

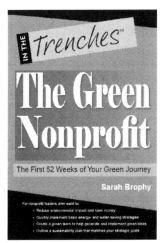

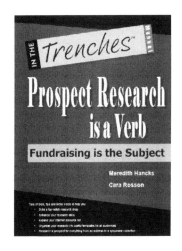

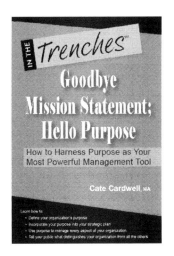

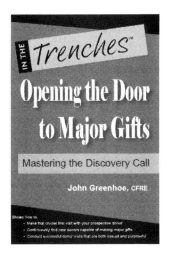

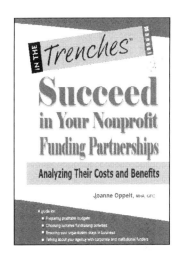

CharityChannel.com/bookstore

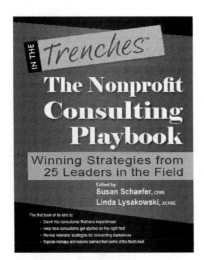

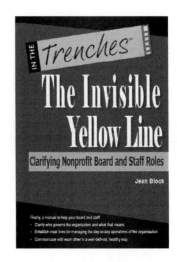

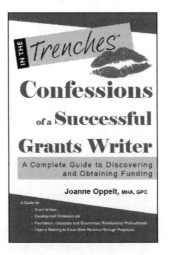

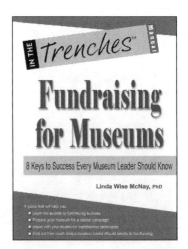

CharityChannel.com/bookstore

And now introducing **For the GENIUS® Press,** an imprint that produces books on just about any topic that people want to learn. You don't have to be a genius to read a **GENIUS** book, but you'll sure be smarter once you do!

ForTheGENIUS.com/bookstore

PRESS

For The GENIUS.com/bookstore

PRESS

Nonprofit Board Service

for the GENIUS®

Find the right board, sharpen your skills, and become a stellar board member

Susan Schaefer, CFRE
Bob Wittig, MBA

FOR THE GENIUS IN ALL OF US™

ForTheGENIUS.com/bookstore

PRESS

Made in the USA
Las Vegas, NV
16 September 2022

55416120R00087